# Unloved

Your Guide To Go From Being **Unloved & Unwanted**
To Fully **Loved & Admired**

## Megan Lis Felix

# 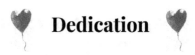 Dedication

As you will read in this book, all I ever wanted was a family, to love and to be loved unconditionally. There were times I thought I forfeited that right, and I would feel unloved forever. Thankfully that is not the truth, and my prayers were answered.

Today, I am loved more than I ever thought possible, and I have a life beyond my wildest dreams. With that being said, I want to dedicate this book to my amazing husband Dr. Eric I. Felix, and my incredible children (and stepchildren) - Mia, Maison, Max, and Gavin.

I love you all more than you know. Eric, thank you for being the best husband and father and thank you for supporting my dreams and investing so much into me. You made *"Unloved"* possible and are playing a big part in leading so many women to freedom.

To our children, you guys are all so very special. I am extremely proud of each of you, and I know you all will do amazing things in this world. Thank you for filling our lives with so much love and happiness. I promise to love you all forever and always!

With all my love,
~Me…

#  Your Survival Guide

# Foreword

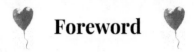

Love – it is the essence of life, the driving force behind our deepest emotions, desires, and dreams. It is the very core of our being, a universal language that transcends time and space. Throughout history, countless songs, stories, and poems have been written in its name, and we all yearn to experience its transformative power. But what happens when, despite our best efforts, we find ourselves staring into the mirror, asking, *"Why don't I feel loved?"*

If you have ever questioned whether you'd find love again, if your parents didn't do their best raising you, or if the wounds of the past have left you undeserving of love, know that you are not alone.

At eighteen years old, after graduating, I found myself trapped in a physically abusive relationship with my first boyfriend, who was two years older than me. This was a time in my life filled with fear, pain, and despair. I endured unimaginable violence and humiliation, as my boyfriend's rage manifested in him pushing me downstairs, trying to suffocate or strangle me, and leaving bruises all over my body as he pulled on my body fat, reminding me that I was "fat and disgusting." It was only through divine intervention and the courage of his own mother, who witnessed his uncontrollable rage and called the police, that I managed to escape this toxic relationship.

In the wake of this harrowing experience, I sought refuge and healing in the most unlikely of places – as a 22-year-old art auctioneer aboard a series of cruise ships. With no formal training and only the guidance of my mentors and my own observations, I used my pain as fuel to be the best and astound the world with my talent, drive, and determination. Yet, even as I achieved success, I was still searching for love in the arms and beds of strangers, only to realize that I was trying to give away something I had never truly possessed.

You see, love has a system. To experience the love we crave, we must understand its true source. As you immerse yourself in *"Unloved"* by Megan Lis Felix, you will discover the key to unlocking the truth about the true Source of love through her own personal story, one that resonates with my own and perhaps yours as well.

Two decades later, after being blessed to coach and mentor thousands of individuals seeking to transform their lives through the power of love, I have found that the most profound breakthroughs are not in finding love but in receiving it.

Embracing love is a decision we must make, acknowledging that the deep wounds of our past are the very gateways to understanding our need for healing and self-compassion.

Megan's story of victory will inspire you to take charge of your life, to realign your identity with your true self, and to embrace the calling that awaits you. It is a tale of overcoming pain and turning it into purpose, walking boldly and generously to share the message of the one true love you seek – not just how to find it but how to receive it, so that you may break the cycle of generational pain and harmful habits, renew your mind, and know that you are loved.

This is your moment of transformation, your opportunity to start anew. When you let love in, you'll experience a change where you'll shift from feeling unloved and unwanted to fully loved and admired because you found the true Source of love - the Source Megan has found, and she openly shares with you. Now, it's your time to begin your journey with *"Unloved,"* and let the power of love change your life forever.

Tara Oldridge
Founder, *Lighthouse Leadership*
Transformational Leadership Coach & Speaker

Unloved

9

#  Letter From The Author

Hello, love!

My name is Megan Felix. I am a wife, a mother, an entrepreneur, and a certified life coach (aka a healing agent). I know what it is like to work hard for everything that you want in life. I also know what it is like to completely lose everything "including yourself" trying to love people that are not capable of loving you. I found myself broken, hopeless, and alone with my three-year-old daughter and finding out I was pregnant with my son. Scared to death of how I would ever recoup or provide for them.

What I didn't know then is this…

Because of all my pain and trauma, I was attracting and allowing people to treat me less than I was worthy of. I had no idea that my fears and focusing on the things I did not want ~ were the exact things I was attracting more of.

It wasn't until I hit bottom that I knew something needed to change. I needed to reprogram my entire way of thinking and being. I began to work with *INSPIRING* women who showed me how to step into my power and change the trajectory for my family.

I want the same for you!

One thing I know for sure is that when we put our healing on the back burner, we bleed all over our children without even realizing it, and my heart hurts for hurting children because I was that child, which is why I have made it my life's mission to share everything I have learned throughout my life.

I created a blueprint in my book *"Unloved"* where I take people through my journey, my healing exercises, and resources that have completely transformed my life.

I believe everyone deserves a life of prosperity and abundance, and it can happen quickly.

Here's to your best life,
~Megan Lis Felix

# Introduction

"You can stay where you are right now and have a mediocre life, or you could take your ring off and lead tens of thousands of women to freedom."

I had a decision to make at that moment. I knew this was God speaking directly to me about where my heart had been and the abundant future He planned for me. But I was here, at a prophetic conference where I was invited to attend the day before by a prophet I met on a street corner that carried a 6-foot cross. I'm *not* kidding.

For weeks leading up to that point, God had been moving my heart to leave my current relationship. He knew I had been settling for a superficial love with my daughter's father because of all the abuse and traumatic events I experienced as a child. To say I felt *unloved* was an understatement.

This superficial love that I settled for did not have any substance to it. To such a degree that I wore a ring, even though I knew deep down in my soul that we would not get married. I never allowed myself to do it because I only wanted to do it once, and I knew that was not where I truly belonged.

And so, here I was being told by God that I could either continue settling for the mediocre life that defined my entire experience on this earth, or I could take my ring off and follow the Holy Spirit into the life of impact that He meant for me to have.

So… *Ring Off!*

As the years passed, it became very clear that God was guiding my every step. I emerged from a broken relationship, uncertain of my path or my future, and emerged as the wife of my soulmate living a life of abundance and prosperity that God had promised me. But that is not all.

God has also blessed me with the power to empower and inspire countless women to rise above their pasts and claim their rightful place in this world, to change the trajectory of their life for themselves and for their children.

Everything God said He would do if I mustered the courage to take my ring off and follow His lead, He has fulfilled in ways I never could have imagined. And here's the good news: He wants to do that for you.

But to claim that life, you must be willing to make a difficult but necessary decision. You must be willing to let go of the things that are holding you back, whether it be unhealthy relationships, the weight of past trauma, or the fear of the unknown. You must choose yourself, and your own well-being, above all else.

Those life-changing blessings and relationships that have your name on it can't be accessed until you have your *"ring off"* moment. Maybe your "ring off" moment isn't actually taking off a physical ring like I did, but maybe it's no longer:

- Trying to love people incapable of loving you
- Spending your time reliving your pain over and over again
- Hurting your children by exposing them to the same abuse or dysfunction you were exposed to
- Refusing to choose yourself first in your life
- Allowing fear of the unknown to hold you back from something greater
- Settling for relationships that no longer serve you

I know what it feels like to grow up without love, to be scarred by violence and trauma, to feel as though there is no hope for a better future. But I also know what it feels like to be loved and cherished, to be surrounded by friends who accept and support you, to live a life of purpose and meaning.

Rising from the ashes of a shattered past, to become a woman of strength, resilience, and grace, is not a feat for the faint of heart. It is a journey of triumph and tribulation, of hope and despair, of joy and sorrow. A journey that I have walked, and one that I am honored to guide you through in these pages.

For years, I wandered aimlessly, lost in the darkness of my own pain and trauma. But with each step, I found the courage to take another, to try again, to hope for a better future. And slowly but surely, I began to heal. To shed the shackles of my past, and to claim the life that was rightfully mine.

And I promise: the same is possible for you.

With this book, I will share with you the secrets of my journey, the wisdom I have gained, the lessons I have learned, and the tools I have used to reclaim my power, my joy, and my love. I will show you how to break free from the chains of your past, and how to rebuild a life of hope and purpose.

This is not a journey that can be rushed, nor one that can be forced. It is a journey of the heart, a journey of the soul, a journey that must be undertaken with care, compassion and patience. But I assure you, it is a journey worth taking.

For when you reach the end of it, you will find yourself standing tall, proud and free, surrounded by love and light. A woman reborn, a woman whole, a woman of unshakable strength and boundless grace.

### _Your Story Is Someone Else's Survival Guide (and this is mine)_

As I stated this guide is not for the faint of heart. It is a call to action, a call to rise up, to claim your power, and to claim your life. A call to break free from the chains of your past and to embrace the healing that you deserve to walk in every day of your life.

In these pages, you will be led on a journey of self-discovery, healing, and growth. A journey that will challenge and push you at times, but one that will bring you to a place of peace, joy, and abundance. Remember even diamonds have to experience pressure but once they go through the process no one can ever take their shine.

In chapter one, you will learn to see your past through new eyes, to understand that it is not a reflection of who you are, but a reflection of something else entirely. This new perspective alone will give you the courage to surrender to the healing process and to embark on this journey with me.

In chapter two, you will make one of the most important decisions of your life, a decision that will melt away all the pain you carry and set you free from the past that has held you captive for so long. This is where true freedom is experienced.

In chapters three and four, you will learn that it does not matter where you come from, or what you've done, you are loved more than you know and there is a *big* and *abundant* life waiting for you. You have a "ring off " moment, and you will discover it here.

In chapter five, I will share the exact tips and actions I took to reprogram my subconscious mind to raise my self-worth. How I went from struggling to get by to experiencing abundance and success in *less* than *six months*.

And in our final chapter, we will explore the abundant, purposeful life that awaits you on the other side of your healing journey. How your divine blessings will find you without you even having to look for them. We will also delve into how your healing will affect your children and your future legacy, because I have learned that God is a generational God, who is thinking about your children and grandchildren more than you do. This is where your legacy is solidified.

One more thing: this journey is not just about reading and understanding. At the end of each chapter, there will be journal questions for you to answer, and process, for even deeper healing. I urge you to make a promise to yourself right now, that you will not move on to the next chapter without completing the journal exercise from the previous chapter. Because this journey is not just about healing, it's about prioritizing yourself before everyone else. It's time for *you* to be first.

So, are you ready? Are you ready to go from feeling unloved and unwanted to fully loved and admired? I acknowledge you for making the decision to heal. I am excited to embark on this journey with you, and I cannot wait to see the amazing woman waiting for you on the other side.

Let's begin…

# Your Past Is Not A Reflection Of You

"It's going to be okay."

As those words of reassurance left my mother's mouth, it was the first time I knew she wasn't telling me the truth. Deep down, I knew everything was *not* going to be okay.

Growing up, all I knew was pain and turmoil. It became so easy for me to feel that something must be wrong because the life I was given was so traumatic. I used to see other people who had some sort of normalcy or stability, and it seemed as though they had it all.

My first memory I could ever recall was around three or four years old. I remember it as if it were yesterday, the first time I was truly introduced to what I would come to know as my childhood. I only know how old I was at the time because of where we were living. This was the first time I felt *unsafe*. My mom and the man that I thought was my father had a very toxic relationship. He was my sister's father and played the role of mine as well. I loved him dearly and in my heart he will always be my dad. We were living in an apartment on the third floor.

I was sitting in the hallway of the building that we lived in, staring out the window towards the parking lot. That's when I saw it - a big black limousine pulling up. The back doors opened and a group of men stepped out, each one armed with a bat or a chain. The atmosphere around me grew tense, as if everyone could sense that something terrible was about to happen. And then they were inside, making their way up the stairs to our floor.

I was frozen in fear, every muscle in my body tense as I heard their footsteps getting closer and closer. I buried my head in my lap, hoping that if I couldn't see them, they couldn't see me. But they walked right past me, the air shifting as they passed. I heard the door to our apartment open, and then the sound of things breaking and walls shaking. I knew they were hurting my dad, and I couldn't do anything to stop it.

The next thing I knew, they were dragging him out of our apartment, his body bruised and bleeding. Once they got down to the second floor, I remember screaming, "Please don't hurt my dad!", but they didn't listen. They took him away and I was left alone, staring out the window and wondering if I would ever see him again. That's when my mother uttered those words I knew weren't true: "It's going to be okay." I remember the day vividly, although I cannot recall the exact date, because of all the emotional shockwaves it sent through my heart and body.

It was unclear how many days had passed when my dad finally returned. His face was bruised, his eyes blackened, and he looked terrible. Anger filled him, and as soon as he entered the house, he immediately went for my mom's purse, taking all the money she had. What followed was a violent fight between them - it was heart-wrenching to see that and hear her screaming, "That's my kids' Christmas money!" He yelled back saying, "There is no f***king Christmas now!"

In a fit of rage that consumed him, he then took our fully decorated Christmas tree and dragged it out of the apartment, down three flights of stairs, and out to the dumpster. Watching our tree go felt like losing a piece of myself went with it. But that was only the beginning - everything escalated from there.

As my dad was disposing of our Christmas tree, my mom began knocking on the neighbors' doors to stop him from taking "her" money. This led to three or four men attacking my dad as he came back into the building, hitting and kicking him mercilessly without any certainty they would stop. *How could this be happening again?!*

I remember standing on the third-floor landing watching the entire thing, crying and screaming, "Stop, you're going to kill him!" That's when someone pulled me back into the apartment and shut the door. This was the second time in a matter of days where I feared I'd never see my dad again or that he'd been killed. But it doesn't end there.

That same night, my dad returned with a vengeance, accompanied by his nephew and their family members in a black van. Their lives were filled with violence because they were heavily involved in the drug trade, so what they did next was normal to them. They proceeded to go to every apartment involved in the prior incident and pulled every single one of those guys that hurt him out of their home and gave them a beating they would never forget. They left their victims lying on the ground, just as they had done to my dad, and drove away like nothing had happened.

They wanted to leave a message that they made a big mistake and should mind their own business from that day forward. For a brief moment, it seemed like everything was over. But the only thing that was over was my mom and dad's relationship.

## *My Only Example Of Love*

Looking back now, I still don't remember if we ever got another tree that year or not, but I do know that we went to my grandmother's every year for Christmas eve thankfully, so we still had a Christmas. She was our saving grace.

As a child, I longed for the holidays, not because of the presents of Christmas or the turkey of Thanksgiving, but because of my grandmother's house. It was a sanctuary, a place of safety where I felt enveloped by the love of a woman who had a heart as big as the world. She never failed to go above and beyond during the holidays, baking cookies for the neighborhood and feeding anyone who came through her door. It was in her presence that I learned what love was, what it truly meant to give of oneself without expectation or reservation.

Even now, the holidays still hold a special meaning, because every Thanksgiving and Christmas without fail, I would see this living embodiment of love on display and in action. There wasn't one holiday season I missed growing up where we weren't at my grandmother's house being loved deeply and inspired to do the same with others.

My grandmother had a special quality, something that I couldn't quite put my finger on. Despite the painful and difficult life she had led, there was a sense of peace and gentleness about her that was very angelic. Her presence brought a sense of calm, and her words were infused with wisdom and kindness. I looked up to her with reverence, and I knew that I was lucky to have her in my life.

She was definitely my angel. She embodied love, and was the only example of it that I had growing up. She lived a life full of dysfunction and pain, but she never let that pain take root in her. I don't know much about her childhood, but I do know that her husband served in World War II and that he was one of the few who made it home alive.

However, back then, people didn't talk about their pain or emotions, so he kept everything bottled up inside and turned to whisky as his only outlet. He drank every day, and when he had enough, he became angry and abusive. My grandmother worked hard to take care of their four children and their home, but it was a constant struggle to provide for them and to make sure everyone felt loved.

Despite all the heartache and pain she experienced, my grandmother somehow always led with love. I cannot imagine how she felt inside throughout her marriage, especially after losing her three-year-old daughter. One day, her daughter came home from the babysitter's house feeling unwell, and my grandmother thought it was just a stomach bug.

However, when she woke up the next morning, she found her baby girl lying in her bed, lifeless and cold. It turned out that the child had ingested some form of cleaner while at the babysitter's house. Now, what would make her do that? Well, my grandfather's whisky was stored under the sink where the babysitter's cleaner was kept. The little girl had seen her father drink from the bottle and thought she was supposed to follow his example.

Instead of resenting her husband and blaming him for their daughter's death, my grandmother chose to be different. She chose to see the good in everything and everyone and became an extremely strong woman who did the best she could under difficult circumstances. I know she likely experienced depression and internal pain due to raising her children with an alcoholic and sometimes abusive husband. However, she never lost sight of what was truly important: love.

I believe that it was the pain in her experiences that led her to build a deep relationship with "God". Whatever it was that she found, it brought her comfort and peace. Because of that, she loved the way she did and became the only place of safety I possessed growing up.

### *Is Anyone There For Me?*

A few years after that traumatic experience with my dad, I'm in first grade and there's a Christmas concert happening at my school. We were singing "Rudolph the Red-Nosed Reindeer" and I was excited because it felt like a huge deal with the weeks we spent practicing on a stage to get it right. Everyone's parents were coming and I asked my mother to come too. I begged and pleaded until she relented, promising that she would be there. I probably asked so much that she just said, "Okay, I'll be there" so I would stop asking.

After weeks of anticipation, the day finally arrives. As the time to begin drew closer, we began to approach the stage. I can still remember standing there, surrounded by my classmates who were smiling and full of joy. Their parents were in the audience, taking pictures and beaming with pride.

I started to lose hope as the minutes passed. I looked everywhere and slowly began to realize in my heart that she wasn't coming.  I started asking myself: Why wasn't I good enough for her to be there for me? Was something wrong with me? At that moment, I began to doubt everything about myself.

As I stood on stage, surrounded by happy, smiling faces, I searched the crowd for my mother, hoping she would surprise me and show up, but she was nowhere to be found. The minutes dragged on, and my hope began to fade. The weight of my disappointment grew heavy, and I felt an ache in my chest and a knot in my throat that I couldn't shake. Everyone else had someone there for them, but me. Instead of my nose just being red, my eyes were too, as they filled up with tears. I started asking myself, "Why wasn't I good enough for someone to be there for me?" Anyone at all would have sufficed. That was the moment my thoughts shifted from, "Something is wrong with my life." to "Something must be wrong with *me*."

### *The Unexpected Gifts These Experiences Gave Me*

After a lot of growth, healing, and understanding, I *now* believe that there is something good in everything, if we look hard enough. It was not always like that, but the truth is that there really is something good in everything and it is our job to find it. What's bad in your experiences are always available to look at, but the "freedom" comes when we can find the good.

1.  Watching the tree get thrown away by my dad actually created a special love for Christmas trees in my heart. I can't explain it but I *love* Christmas trees and I would have one up all year if I could. The lights and the way they illuminate the room represent such a lasting sense of peace for me.

2.  I was able to realize how badly it hurts to not have anyone show up for me. Because of that intense pain, I promised myself I would never miss anything like that for my children. The pain of being unloved as a child caused me to be an even greater mother to my own children. At the time of this writing, I recently just flew home a few days early to make sure I did not miss my daughter's school concert.

As I shared at the beginning of our journey together, experiencing the healing to go from feeling unloved and unwanted to fully loved and admired will require you to do more than just reading this, if you want to create anything new in your life. As I'm sure you have heard, "Knowing is only *half* of the battle." Knowledge is not enough. It takes real work and unfortunately, that word causes resistance in some people.

It does not have to be that way though. We can change the way we look at anything in an instant. Here's a powerful lesson I've learned that's changed my life and I know will change yours if you let it: when we change the way we look at things, *the things we look at change.* The work that it is going to take for you to heal and create the life of your dreams is actually *not* work at all - it is an opportunity. It's an opportunity for you to see how life happens *for* us and not *to* us.

Finding a gift or lesson in any adversity you face is a very healthy exercise that can set you free in an instant. The first step to going from feeling unloved and unwanted to fully loved and admired is embracing the truth that your past is not a reflection of you. Just because something was done to you doesn't mean it has the power to define you or devalue you.

Think about it like this: Imagine I have a $100 bill in my hand and I want to give it to you. Now before I hand it over, envision that I crumbled it until it got so small you couldn't see it. Then right before I give it to you, I then throw it on the ground and begin stepping on it at least five times.

2. The second situation is:

_____

_____

_____

The gift in that situation is:

_____

_____

_____

3. The third situation is:

_____

_____

_____

The gift in that situation is:

_____

_____

_____

# Releasing The Pain They Caused

"Take it back!"

Those were the words that came out of my sister's mouth as she saw my mom holding me for the first time. She couldn't understand what happened because my mom never told anyone that she was pregnant with me, including my sister. I now know she didn't tell anyone because she was scared and probably never came to terms with herself that she was pregnant.

When my sister found out, she was 7 years old at the time and all she remembers is my mom leaving with a suitcase and coming home a few days later with a baby. I'm sure it wasn't easy for her because at first she was the complete focus of everyone, and all of a sudden, I am taking the attention away from her. She mentioned that all I would do was cry and my grandmother would just rock me for hours.

My sister resented me from the start and never chose to hide that from me. She would tell me any chance she could that nobody wanted me, so I was left on the doorstep and they brought me inside because my grandmother felt sorry for me.

Some people would mention that she was only joking but to a child that already feels unwanted and unloved, those are devastating words.

My young heart could never understand why my hero and idol, my sister, hated me so much. She was the one I wanted to be like. I went everywhere she went and did everything she did. But I was just a burden to her that she had to continually watch and babysit.

I wasn't a stranger to being the target of her unresolved pain. She thought crying was a weakness and made fun of me every time I cried. Since I have always felt things deeply as a child, I cried a lot. My face is also very active so when I cried my forehead would wrinkle up. One day I was in the dining room and was really distraught about something. My mom and my sister were laughing at me and somehow came up with this nickname, "Wrinkle Dinkle". That was my name for years.

At first it hurt, but after a while it started to just make me angry on the inside. My sister did not cry, instead she would just take her frustration and anger out on me. Because she was a lot bigger than me and really strong, whenever I made her mad, which I did a lot, she would just start punching me. She was 5'11 when I was seven and hit like a man. These beatings over time formed the false belief within my heart that *love hurts*. I could never understand how someone could be so cold towards me when I loved them so much.

Even though my sister was never one to show much kindness, one day, she surprised me by bringing back two stuffed dolls from her vacation. They were a boy and a girl doll, and I remember feeling overwhelmed with gratitude and love. In that moment, it seemed as though my sister had thought of me, and maybe even cared for me, after all. I held those dolls close to my heart, and they brought me an immense amount of comfort and joy. It was as though they were a symbol of the affection and love that I had always longed for from my sister. To keep them safe, we placed them back in a bag and walked it down to the garage assigned to us. Everyone that lived in the neighborhood was assigned a separate garage and they were all located next to one another at the bottom of the neighborhood.

It wasn't easy for me growing up to experience pain up close from someone I deeply loved. Her actions, driven by her own pain, left an indelible mark on my young heart. Unbeknownst to me, I was soon to cross paths with someone who would inflict pain on me for the sheer pleasure of it.

*Unloved*

## *Hello, Jimmy*

Jimmy's presence in my life marked the beginning of my
experience with a toxic relationship and the world of bullying.
Being the tender age of seven years old, his cruel acts towards me
started with sabotaging my bike—locking the handlebars and
severing the brake line—so that I'd lose control speeding down
the hill and collide directly into a tree. I still recall my sister
carrying me home and placing me in a bathtub that swiftly turned
red from the blood I'd shed.

He just laughed, as though it was all a joke. Then he
tried to convince me that my bike must have been faulty and that
he would never do such a thing. I wanted to believe him, to
continue playing with him, even though my instincts told me he
was lying. It was strange—when we were alone, he was genuinely
kind to me, and I craved that affection. I had no other friends,
having recently moved to the area and not knowing a soul.

Sometime later, Jimmy was playing football, and I asked
if I could join. Alone, he would toss the ball gently and treat me
kindly, but everything changed when others were around. I
missed a pass, not even seeing the ball coming. He stood before
me and hurled the football right at my face with all his might.

Tears streamed down my cheeks as I cried out in pain, but he only laughed and taunted me for being a crybaby. Logic would dictate that I should have stayed far away from him, never speaking to him again. And yet, I tried, only to find out that he didn't need to hurt me physically to cause me pain.

During the darkest days of the bullying I endured, I learned just how twisted and cruel Jimmy could be. One day I was riding my bike with my friend Jessica, we were riding down the street pretending to drive different types of cars. I imagined myself driving a purple Chevy Camaro with AM/FM radio (that was a big deal back then), and we were having a great time until we turned a corner. Suddenly, my world came crashing down, and my heart sank. I was frozen in shock, unable to comprehend who could do something so terrible and why.

There, hanging from a tree, were the two beloved dolls my sister had given me from her vacation, the ones that meant the world to me because they became one of my only signs of love from her. They were not merely dismantled, but utterly destroyed. Their limbs had been hacked off, their bodies stained with black marks, as if they were beat up with a stick. Worst of all, they hung from their necks, the rope tied with a precision that made it clear this had been a deliberate, evil act.

As I stood there, trying to process what I was seeing, a sickening realization dawned on me: *Jimmy had done this.* He had taken the only things that gave me solace and obliterated them, just to hurt me. The cruelty of his act was unfathomable, and it left me reeling with pain and confusion. Even now, as I live this abundant life I've been gifted with, I still struggle to make sense of Jimmy's actions. How could someone be so twisted, so devoid of empathy or compassion, that they would take pleasure in destroying something so innocent and cherished?

To some, it might seem trivial to care so deeply about some dolls that my sister gave me, but I couldn't help having such a big heart at a young age. My heart ached for everything more than I wanted it to. I often tried to convince myself not to care about certain things, even pretending at times that I was indifferent. Yet, I could never find myself being comfortable with faking it.

For three long years, I endured this torment, each day becoming a relentless cycle. The pain was challenging to bear, especially as it came from someone who occasionally showed me kindness, only to severely bully me at other times. Little did I know that a few years later, I would face an even greater heartache when I lost one of my closest friends.

## *She Never Made It Back*

There's one experience at eight years old that shook me to my core and showed me that evil does exist and it can be closer than you think. One day I came outside in the morning to go to school and when I opened the door and stepped out I could feel a sense of coldness that I had never felt before. It is almost indescribable. The air was different and you could feel the heaviness in the atmosphere. I knew something was terribly wrong.

The night before I was playing in the park across the street with two other girls, April and Brenda, like we always did. I considered them my best friends. We literally did everything together and were with each other every day. They were like my family. There was also a kid in the neighborhood named Joey who was seven years older than us, but that didn't stop him from coming to the park every day to play with us. He pushed us on the swings and made us feel like we were cool. He acted like he really cared about us and said he was like a brother to us. We trusted him, and so did everyone else.

With it getting dark, we all needed to go home and Brenda lived on the other street. Since it was getting late, Joey offered to walk her home. I lived right across the street and April lived close by too, so we walked home on our own. We all said goodnight and planned when we would meet at the bus stop in the morning. We all went home as usual, not suspecting a thing.

The next morning, everything was different. The air felt heavy, and there were more cops and emergency vehicles than we had ever seen before. The streets were blocked off, and even the schools were shut down. Here's the shocking truth of what happened that night: *Brenda never made it home!*

It turned out that Joey had done something sickening and animalistic to her. We were all horrified. Nothing like this had ever happened in our area before, and it was almost impossible to comprehend. The police found Brenda's body mutilated on a rock in the woods that we played in before. That boy strangled her with an extension cord and did unthinkable things to her body that are only reserved in a horror movie.

I couldn't fathom why or how something so terrible could happen. We were all eight years old, and he had taken our innocence away. People would talk about God around me and I thought, *"If there was a God, why didn't He protect her?"*

He had also taken a part of Brenda's brothers that day. They wanted nothing more than to hurt him like he had hurt her, and they did everything they could think of to get themselves sent to jail. Joey hurt us all that night, and he didn't even know how much. He robbed Brenda and everyone who loved her, and it was hard to see how we all could ever recover from such a tragedy.

### *Another One Gone*

How to get through losing one of your best friends in that way is not easy, but how I handled Brenda being taken from us was leaning on my other best friend, April. We spent every second together after that and it felt like we were at each other's houses all the time. But that did not last long.

All of a sudden, a few years after we lost Brenda, we were separated with both of our families forbidding us to ever interact with each other. What happened during that time? Well, she had an older brother that was my sister's age. He was always really nice to all of the girls in the neighborhood and was even friends with my sister. Since I spent the night at her house frequently, he became extra nice to me and would play with us a lot. At first, I liked the attention he paid towards me because I felt so unloved throughout my life. That's when things started to progress where he began to touch me in ways that I knew were not normal.

He would often play with my hair, hug me tightly for a long time, and sometimes even ask me to sit on his lap while he told me how beautiful I was. Occasionally, he would even kiss my neck while hugging me. I knew in my heart that something was off, and that what he was doing was not right. However, I didn't fully understand what was going on. It was a confusing situation because although I knew it was wrong, he would tell me, "Relax, it's okay. This is what a boy does when he loves a girl.

"Nooo, stop."

That's all I could to say as a twelve-year-old girl to a nineteen-year-old boy. Tears filled my eyes and he tried to console me with apologies. Deep down, I found myself feeling conflicted. He told me he couldn't help himself, that I was too beautiful and that he loved me. A part of me wanted to believe him, desperately hoping that he wasn't a bad person and that what he had done was somehow justified. But I knew deep down that what had happened was wrong, and that he had hurt me.

What made things even worse was the fear of losing my best friend April, his sister, if I ever spoke out about what had happened. The mere thought of losing her was unbearable, as I loved her more than anything since we already lost Brenda to an accident so horrific. So, I resorted to the only coping mechanism I knew - I tried to convince myself that what had happened was normal. Maybe it was what grown-ups do, I thought, and shoved the memories into the "block out box" in my mind. For a brief moment, it seemed like it was working. But eventually, the reality of what had occurred started to seep through the cracks, and one way or another it was coming out.

"Get the f*ck in the bathroom."

It started with a single command from my sister. That was the moment everything changed. I knew that I had to obey my sister, or else I would have been dragged in there against my will. But I had no idea what was about to happen.

As I entered the bathroom, she started hitting me, punching me in the back of the head repeatedly. This was not new to me, though I usually knew what it was for; but this time I had absolutely no idea what I had done wrong. Through the pain and confusion, I screamed, "What's going on?!" "Why are you hitting me?!" All my sister had to do was mention his name - that's when I felt my heart stop for a minute.

I couldn't believe what was happening. *How did it come to this?* I could only cry all the tears I had in my heart and murmur the words "I told him Nooooo. Please stop hitting me." My sister finally stopped and demanded an explanation. In between gasps for air, I tried to explain as best she could, but I couldn't.

Soon after, my worst fears came true. My sister immediately told my mother, who was screaming and freaking out. I was always afraid of this moment - the moment when my mother found out. I was afraid that she would no longer allow me to be friends with April anymore. My mother calls her mother and starts screaming at her. In the midst of all this happening, I couldn't help but let out a shrieking scream of pain. My world had just ended, again. The same feeling came back, one I couldn't shake off - it's the one I had when I found out that Brenda was gone and I would never see her again.

To make matters worse, I had to go into a courtroom and sit there as attorney's asked me a bunch of questions. To top it off, he sat in front of me looking directly at me. My heart was pounding in my chest. I was terrified and felt sick to my stomach. Sitting down where they told me to, I tried to avoid looking at anyone or anything. I was completely numb, a shell of a person. When someone started asking me questions, I froze. I just shook my head 'yes' and 'no', trying not to make things any worse.

All I could think about was my best friend, her family, and what they would think of me. I prayed that his mom would see that I wasn't trying to get her son in trouble, that I just wanted everything to go away and go back to the way it was before. I wanted my friend back, but deep down inside I knew it wasn't possible. When the verdict came, I should have been happy that he was going away for a few years, but I wasn't. I was sad because I knew I would never be able to have my friend back. Her family would hate me forever, and I would never be allowed to talk to her again.

It wasn't fair. She had nothing to do with what happened, and she couldn't do anything to change him. I knew she would have if she could have. But the reality was that my family would never want me to be friends with her again. It felt like I was being punished for something that wasn't my fault. It was a nightmare that I couldn't wake up from. I could not understand how or why this was happening. This continual question kept circulating inside of my head: *Why did I have to lose another friend?*

### *The Truth Comes Out*

Years later, I couldn't help but feel like everything good in my life was gone. My grandmother, the only source of unconditional love I had ever known, had passed away, and the pain was starting to turn to anger. I was just so mad at the world.

To make matters worse, the man who I thought was my dad was an alcoholic and drunk pretty much every day. I had been spending more time at my grandparents' house so my grandfather wouldn't be alone, and one day, I saw the ice cream truck coming down the street. Excited, I ran up to my dad and asked him for money to buy an ice cream. But he turned around and said, "No, I don't have it." I couldn't help but retort, "You have money for beer." I didn't end it there, "You're just a drunk alcoholic." That's when he slapped me across the face. I ran inside the house, crying.

My mom came to get me, and when we got home, she sat me down at the table and said, "He had no business hitting you. He's not your father, anyway." *WHAT?!* My heart sank to the floor. This couldn't be happening. *Does that mean my sister isn't my sister, either?* Despite everything she had done to me, I still loved her more than anything.

"So, who is my father?" I asked. "A man who tried to abort you," she replied. "When I told him I was pregnant, he took me to New York to get an abortion. But when we got there, I couldn't go through with it. I never spoke to him again."

I was in complete shock. I had so many questions. Thoughts of my own father trying to kill me raced through my mind, and I felt completely worthless as a twelve-year-old girl. They say if you want to overwhelm your mind, then ask yourself multiple deep questions in a row without giving yourself time to answer them. That's exactly what I did.

I wondered to myself, *Would my mom and sister even care if I was gone? Would they be happy they didn't have to deal with me anymore?* These were the conversations I had with myself. That night, as I laid in bed, I prayed to God, "If You're real, *don't* let me wake up tomorrow." When I woke up the next morning, I told myself that God must not be real because I was still here. After all, if He was a loving God, why would He give me *this* life?

I didn't know how to release any of the pain, and I had been programmed not to tell anyone about the things that happened at home, so I kept everything inside of me. The pain had turned to anger, which was now turning to hate. I hated my life, I hated myself, and I hated everything around me.

Instead of me being hurt by other people by being weak, I started getting in trouble all the time at school, and I fought a lot. I built walls and subconsciously kept anyone from getting close to me. I developed a belief system ("BS") that created beliefs within me like "*If I don't let you in, you can't hurt me*". Here's the truth: I was just a hurt little girl who wanted to be loved.

## *Your Second Step*

Forgiveness is a powerful tool that can help you find freedom from the pain and hurt of the past. Although some experiences may seem unforgivable, it's important to take another look. Picturing yourself outside of the situation allows you to see more than just your pain, and when you finally see more than just *your* pain, that's when you have the greatest opportunity for your pain to be healed. That leads me to share with you one of the most powerful truths I've ever come across: *we begin in pain because of a situation, but we stay in pain because we focus on ourselves.*

You see, people only do what was done to them and treat people the way that they were once treated. That's why the old adage consistently turns out to be true over time: *hurt people, hurt people.* And even if the treatment they experienced wasn't intentional by the other person, it is their *interpretation* of how they were treated that truly matters the most. When our inner self listens from a place of hurt or pain, we can take in things that were not originally intended to be received that way.

For example, with my best friend's brother: someone may have touched him in ways that were inappropriate and hurt him as a child. Now you could argue that he should have known better, and I don't disagree with you. However, because I understand that *hurt people, hurt people*, I can forgive him freely knowing that his actions no longer have a hold on my heart.

Looking back, I realize now that my mom was doing the best she could with what she had. She had her own pain and struggles to carry, and she was doing her best to navigate through them. I used to be angry at her for some of the choices she made, but now I understand that sometimes we don't have more than the options that are given to us.

Forgiveness is not just about others, but also about giving permission to ourselves. It's about releasing the weight of anger and pain that we carry within us and giving ourselves permission to heal. So, I choose to forgive my mom and let go of the hurt that was holding me back. It's not always easy, but it's worth it. When we forgive, we can finally break free from the chains that have bound us and move forward with grace and love.

Because the second step to going from feeling unloved and unwanted to fully loved and admired is to *release the pain they caused you*, I want you to take a moment to think of at least two experiences from your past that still hurt you. Write them down on a piece of paper and then close your eyes and ask this question out loud, "What could have happened to them that caused them to behave like this?" "Were they abused, neglected, or rejected in some way?"

When you get an answer, write it down. This exercise can help you see the reasons behind their actions and give you a deeper understanding of the situation. The more people you can do this for and forgive, the more freedom you'll experience.

Now that you can see how someone could have hurt you, you can start to forgive. The freedom you deserve and the life you've envisioned is on the other side of releasing the pain that's actually holding onto you. If you do not learn to forgive, *your healing journey will end here.*

The first experience I want to let go of is:

_____

_____

_____

What could have happened to them is:

_____

_____

_____

(Repeat this part out loud)

_____, I forgive you for

_____

_____

_____

and I willingly release this situation. (Repeat this statement out loud)

The second experience I want to let go of is:

_____

_____

_____

What could have happened to them is:

_____

_____

_____

*Unloved*

(Repeat this part out loud)

_____, I forgive you for

_____

_____

_____

and I willingly release this situation.  (Repeat this statement out loud)

#  Giving Yourself A New Story

"Thank you for sharing that. I've been carrying the same
secret with me my entire life."

For a long time, I kept a secret that I never thought I'd
share publicly. It was something I had buried so deep inside that
I assumed it would remain hidden forever, even coming with me
to the grave. I was quite hard on myself about it and couldn't
imagine telling anyone, not even my husband. Initially, I didn't
plan to include it in this book, but I realized how important it
was to share, so the book went through a complete rewrite to
ensure it was no longer a secret. It happened by accident.

The reason this secret came to light was due to a training
I attended recently with *Lighthouse Leadership*. It was during one of
our close-knit sharing sessions that the secret unexpectedly
surfaced.

"Everyone, take a moment to share your life's story with
your buddy," our group leader instructed. "You have two
minutes to describe your life's journey to your partner." Caught
off guard by the sudden request, I found myself unprepared for
the task at hand, but I called Kylie anyway.

As I began to speak, I felt the words pouring out of me, a cascade of memories that included a secret I had never shared with anyone. I had meant to keep it locked away, but it slipped out of my mouth like a shadow from the deepest corner of my mind.

To my surprise, I didn't even realize I had shared the secret until it was Kylie's turn to share her story. Her heart cracked wide open, tears streamed down her cheeks as her voice trembled, "Thank you for sharing that. I've been carrying the same secret with me my entire life." My revelation had given Kylie permission to heal, to forgive herself, and to move forward.

It was then that I knew God wanted me to include the secret in this book. A couple of days later, I confided in my husband over dinner, and then reached out to Christian, my ghostwriter, to discuss adding it back into the manuscript. It had been there initially, but I removed it in a moment of doubt.

Sharing my secret brought me relief, empowerment, and freedom. It felt like breaking free from a cage, liberated from the internal torment and self-doubt that had weighed me down. This experience taught me a valuable lesson: *Those unhealed parts of ourselves will always linger, threatening to resurface if they aren't confronted and released.*

## *The Secret Revealed*

It is no coincidence that as I entered adulthood, I attracted toxic and sometimes abusive relationships because we attract what we know, so I found myself in a really abusive relationship when I was younger. I was with a man that was mentally, emotionally, and sometimes even physically abusive and I stayed because at the time, that was what I had experienced as a child and believed this was the normal expression of love. I somehow was not careful enough and found myself pregnant at nineteen years old.

I promised myself as a child that I would never allow my children to be subjected to the pain and dysfunction that I had been and I knew if I had that baby, they would have gone through the same things. I was so scared and so lost and had no idea what to do. So, I did the only thing I knew to do at the time and that was to *not go through with the pregnancy*.

It was one of the hardest and most agonizing decisions I have ever made in my life. I remember feeling a heavy weight on my chest, as if the world was closing in on me. The shame and guilt consumed me, suffocating me. I felt like a failure as a woman, as a mother. I felt like I had let my child down before they even had a chance to take their first breath.

I tried to bury the pain, to lock it away in a box and pretend it never happened, but the memories haunted me. They clawed at me in my sleep and followed me during my waking hours. I wondered if I had made the right choice.

## *The Aftermath*

You see, all I ever wanted was a child, and as I look back on those dark years that followed, I realize now that my desperation for a child was born out of a deeper longing for love and acceptance. I wanted someone to love me unconditionally, the way I loved my own mother despite all her flaws.

But as the years passed, something happened that almost shattered that dream: *my period ceased.* Here I was, 27 years old, a business owner sitting in my apartment feeling empty on the inside. On top of that, with the problems of my period, I was afraid that I might never experience the joy of motherhood, and with it, the love that I so desperately craved.

As I searched for answers, I went from doctor to doctor, trying every vitamin and medication known to man, but nothing seemed to work. I began to question whether I was being punished by God for what I did. It's strange how we often turn to a higher power when things go wrong, but when things are going well, we rarely acknowledge one. I too was guilty of this, and I felt like I was being robbed of a chance to experience the one thing that would give my life meaning.

The weight of the fear and uncertainty was crushing. The idea of not being able to experience a love as pure and unconditional as a child's was suffocating. It felt like my biological clock was ticking down to zero, and with each passing day, my self-worth dwindled. I was convinced that if I didn't have a child by 30, then I would have failed as a woman, as a mother. Seeing friends and family members happily starting families only intensified my anxiety and shame. I was desperate to experience that, too, to feel the same love they possessed, but it felt like I gave up that right with my decision.

To make matters worse, I felt trapped in my own mind. The messages I received growing up about not sharing personal struggles only reinforced my isolation. It was like a vicious cycle of self-doubt and self-judgment, where the more I kept my pain to myself, the more it ate away at me. Those conversations with myself were terrible. Self-defeating questions like, *"What is wrong with you?"* and *"Why would you do that?"* echoed through my mind almost every day.

So, I buried it deep, hoping that if I ignored it long enough, it would disappear. But the pain and emptiness remained, festering inside me, waiting for an opportunity to resurface. It was a defense mechanism, a way to protect myself from feeling the unbearable pain, but it only made the situation worse. If the cycle of guilt didn't bring me to my lowest place, what happened during Thanksgiving that year would.

### ***Breakdown To Breakthrough***

"I don't know what to tell you. Figure it out."

CLICK.

As if it happened only yesterday, the memory of those piercing words still echoes in my mind. The clicking sound of my mother hanging up on me felt like a physical blow to my heart, and I struggled to catch my breath. With the holidays approaching, a time of year that held so much meaning for me, I found myself in a lonely and desolate place.

Every year, I spent Thanksgiving with my mom and my grandmother - when she was alive, but this year was different.

Driving home from my shop, I received a call from her. My heart leapt with joy, but that joy quickly turned to shock and despair as she informed me that she would be spending the holiday with Rich's family. She really chose Rich, her boyfriend, over her own daughter. I was stunned and devastated. Tears streamed down my face as I asked her, "What about me?! Where can I go?" I begged her to reconsider, but her response was cold and heartless, "I don't know what to tell you. Figure it out." And with that, she hung up. CLICK.

I felt like I had been punched in the gut. How could a mother not care and leave her child alone on such an important day? I was overwhelmed with feelings of abandonment, rejection, and unworthiness. I felt unloved, and the pain inside me had become so unbearable that as soon as I walked into my apartment, I collapsed on the floor, crying so hard that the neighbors across the street could have heard me. I grabbed a pillow and screamed into it, hoping that the muffled sounds would prevent anyone from hearing my pain.

This was the first time I ever gave myself permission to let it out. I had always been more worried about what people would think of me, but this time I didn't care. I was alone, and the pain was so great to bear, all I could do in that moment was cry out, "God, if You are real, please take this from me!"

As I let out another loud cry, something very different happened. I felt a presence enveloping me, and a voice whispering, *"It's okay. I've got you."* It was a feeling that I couldn't deny, a sense of comfort that I had never felt before. In that moment, I realized that I was never truly alone.

"I'm sorry," I whispered, my voice hoarse from the tears. "I was scared and just wanted to protect them."

*"I know,"* He replied. *"It's okay, I've got you."*

I felt as though something was hugging me, holding me tight and comforting me like the father I didn't have. It was an experience words couldn't describe, and for the first time in my life, I truly believed that everything would be okay. His voice brought such a sense of peace that as it washed over me, I actually began to feel a sense of excitement inside. It was as though life was being poured back into me, and I started having visions of me doing amazing things in this life. For the first time in my life, I experienced a freedom on the inside I didn't even know existed.

His words continued to echo in my heart, *"I am your Father and I have always been there for you. You are My child and I LOVE you. I have amazing plans for you. Everything you went through has a purpose. It wasn't about you at all."*

That night, as I lay in bed, I couldn't help but envision myself speaking on stages all around the world. I almost didn't sleep all night. The excitement in my heart was palpable, and I knew that my life had meaning and would never be the same. To feel hope for my future made my experience so real and intimate that I knew I could no longer deny there was a God. To top it all off, after one full year of not having my period, it came back *three days later.*

Looking back from the abundant life I live right now, I realize that life is happening *for* you, and not *to* you. That pain I went through was necessary for me to experience this powerful moment of breakthrough. If my mom hadn't left for Thanksgiving, I would have never reached the breaking point that brought me to my knees. The moment of your greatest breakdown has the potential to become the moment of your greatest breakthrough, if you let it.

## *Your Third Step*

In the previous chapter, we discussed the importance of forgiving others, but that's just the first step in the forgiveness process. The next step is forgiving ourselves, letting go of the past mistakes that weigh heavily on our minds and hearts. If we don't do that, we'll continue to repeat the cycle because that's who we believe we really are. And remember this: *we always become what we believe about ourselves.* Today is your day to finally let go of your past mistakes, to finally stop allowing them to eat away at you and come out in destructive ways.

If that means calling out to God in a private moment and pouring out your heart to Him, then do it. Close this book right now and have your moment with Him. He doesn't care what you've done, where you've been, or what you think about yourself. He loves you unconditionally and wants to heal your heart completely, like He did with me in my breakthrough moment.

Whatever you've heard about God, if it's negative, just know that religion may have distorted the truth about Him. I've learned that condemnation doesn't come from Him, it comes from us or the enemy. So right now, I invite you to experience Him for yourself without any outside influences altering the truth about what He's really like. I promise you, He already knows everything you've done, and still loves you anyway. No matter what you've been through, or what you may have done, He still loves you. I believe He had me share my secret with you to show you that I broke one of the worst commandments, but He doesn't look at our mistakes, He looks at our heart. He just wants us to grow to *know* and *love* Him so we can learn to grow and *love* others.

Because the third step to going from feeling unloved and unwanted to fully loved and admired is to *give yourself a new empowering story*, we are going to embark on a self-forgiveness exercise that has the power to transform your entire life. If you're feeling comfortable with this, invite God to join you on this journey. I highly recommend it, but I also understand that not everyone is ready for that just yet. Find a peaceful and quiet spot, away from all distractions.

First, lean back and gently close your eyes. Take a few deep breaths, choosing to smell the roses with each inhale and blowing out candles with each exhale. Although it may come naturally to some, for many of us, including myself, breathing deeply was not something we knew how to do. My nervous system was always in a state of fight or flight for the first 33 years of my life, so I never learned how to breathe properly and relax my body. But trust me when I say that the breakthrough happens in that relaxed state, and those long, deep breaths are the key to unlocking it.

Secondly, place both hands on your heart and sit up straight, or if you prefer, stand tall. Make sure your spine is elongated and breathe deeply, allowing the oxygen to flow into your back. You'll feel your spine opening up with every inhale.

Now it's time for the self-forgiveness exercise. Start by thinking of something you need to forgive yourself for, like hurting someone or breaking the law. Then, follow it up with asking, "What is the truth about yourself?" It'll be one that empowers you, because if it's not, then it's not the truth. *The truth sets you free, while lies lock you in a cage.*

For instance, "What I forgive myself for is that I hurt someone's feelings, but the truth about me is that I have a good heart and always strive to do better." This is your chance to give yourself a new, empowering story. A story that will lift you up and propel you towards feeling fully loved.

With both hands on your heart and your spine stretched as tall as it can be, ask the question out loud: *"What do I need to forgive myself for?"*

_____

_____

_____

_____

Let the answer come to you, trusting that it will surface from within. You keep your eyes closed, not wanting to disrupt this peaceful state.

As the answer reveals itself, hold it in your mind and ask the next question out loud: *"What is the truth about me?"*

Or, if you want to ask God, you can ask Him: *"What is the truth about who I really am in Your eyes?"*

_____

_____

_____

_____

Now read it out loud and follow it with this statement: "I willfully release any pain or trauma this has caused me."

Last question to ask yourself: *"With my new story, what are two decisions I can make today that will align my life with this truth?"*

_____

_____

_____

_____

You can do this exercise with as many "things" as you would like.

As you close this chapter of your journey towards healing and growth, take a moment to reflect on how far you have come. You have faced your fears and vulnerabilities, and you have shown yourself the compassion and forgiveness that you deserve. You have taken the courageous steps to release the weight of the past, and to embrace a new, empowering story for yourself.

So, as you turn the page to the next chapter, I want you to carry with you the knowledge that you are capable of healing, growth, and transformation. You are worthy of love and belonging, and you have everything you need within you to create the life you truly desire.

And remember, even in the moments when the journey feels hard, you can always come back to this moment of celebration and self-love. Give yourself a hug and let the warmth of that embrace remind you of your strength, resilience, and endless potential. The world needs your light, God loves you unconditionally, and I believe in you.

Unloved

69

# I Prayed For You

After my *breakdown to breakthrough* moment where a deep, lasting peace filled my heart for the first time and my absent period miraculously returned after a year, I could no longer deny the existence of God. My mother's departure with Rich that Thanksgiving, leaving me to fend for myself only ignited a prayer within me: a desire for a partner to share my life and create the family I had always longed for, one that would love me the way I always yearned to be loved.

As if in an answer to my prayers, Bart entered my life. A childhood friend, he felt like a safe harbor, his kind heart and gentle nature assuring me that he would never harm me or a child. With a genuine love for children, an unwavering work ethic, and a chivalrous demeanor, Bart seemed perfect. He even owned his own house and had recently given up his partying ways.

Blinded by hope, I chose to overlook his heavy need for attention and his history of infidelity, focusing instead on the potential I saw within him. Little did I know, such wishful thinking was a dangerous path.

Things seemed perfect at first, or at least I wanted them to be so badly that I overlooked the imperfections and convinced myself they didn't exist. We were on the same path, and it appeared that God was bringing people and events into our lives to help us grow closer to Him. Bart had a big heart like mine, and if someone was struggling, he would invite them to stay with us and do whatever he could to help.

Our mutual friend Curtis, who we grew up with, faced tough times and battled addiction. After spending a few months in rehab, he returned as a different person. There was something about him that was hard to ignore. He had an irresistible energy, happiness, and freedom.

There was a sparkle in his eyes and an indescribable peace about him that attracted everyone. When he told me that no matter what happened to him in life, he knew he'd be okay, I remember thinking, "I want that... whatever it is, I want it," and Bart felt the same way.

Curtis and I grew even closer, and he often talked to me about various things. We started going to a church called First Baptist with him. He was getting baptized with his daughter and asked me if I would join them. I knew I wanted the peace and happiness that I saw in him, so I gladly accepted the offer, and we got baptized together.

### *Prayers Answered*

Bart and I had been together for some time, and we were eager to have a baby. However, it seemed as if it just wasn't happening. Perhaps I was stressing myself out too much, but one day I finally sought God's help. I was in church on a Sunday, and the sermon discussed the true meaning of Easter. The Easter eggs we associate with the holiday symbolize new life or rebirth.

Although I had celebrated Easter my entire life, I never connected the eggs to the eggs within us women—until that day. The realization struck me powerfully. I sat there, asking God to work a miracle within me and allow me to become pregnant. Remarkably, I felt that He heard me and *it would be done.*

Soon after, I took a pregnancy test, and it came back positive. We were overjoyed. Bart was as eager for a baby as I was. He wanted to be the father he never had while growing up. We both yearned for someone who would love us unconditionally. At this point, I still had my own business and had the opportunity to purchase a building with a three-bedroom apartment above the salon downstairs. This was something I had envisioned and spoken about many times. It would have been a dream come true and spared me from a lot of unnecessary pain.

However, no matter how amazing this opportunity was, I still clung to old fears. There were two fears that held my heart: one, I was afraid of losing my investment and two, more importantly, of failing as a mother. I convinced myself that I couldn't be a full-time business owner and a good mother, which were complete lies that I had believed.

Looking back though, I realize that God was answering my prayers and offering the stability I had always craved. Growing up, I had watched my mom work tirelessly, often to the detriment of our relationship, so it was easy for me to talk myself out of pursuing this opportunity—a decision I would later come to regret.

Bart, who was intent on providing for our family, suggested that I become a stay-at-home mom. Initially, the idea seemed wonderful. I had been working every day since I was 14, so taking a break appeared to be a dream come true. However, I soon discovered that it wasn't at all what I had imagined. Perhaps for a woman with a "normal" life, or someone who didn't grapple with people-pleasing tendencies, struggles with self-identity, and self-worth, it could have been perfect—but I did face those challenges. I also suffered from perfectionism, which meant I spent every day striving to create and maintain an unattainable ideal of "perfect." Despite the impossibility of my goal, I couldn't help but keep trying.

## *Feeling The Need To Contribute*

From childhood, I believed I had to earn money to avoid feeling like a burden. I didn't want to ask for anything, as it often led to disappointment. Despite agreeing to be a stay-at-home mom, I sought ways to contribute financially. I decided to babysit for friends with a baby the same age as our daughter. Soon, I realized caring for two infants was harder than I thought, and I questioned my abilities.

Every day was spent cleaning, taking care of babies, cooking, and tending to other chores. With my perfectionism, I couldn't sleep unless everything was spotless. I was constantly giving to others, leaving nothing for myself. Exhausted, I'd lock myself in the bathroom and cry, feeling utterly depleted. Simple tasks seemed monumental, and even showering was a challenge with one or both babies crying. I knew I couldn't continue like this, so I stopped babysitting and enrolled our daughter in daycare.

I felt like I was losing my identity. Accustomed to working and staying active, I didn't know who I was anymore. *I used to have really big dreams, but my only dream at that moment was to have a day or two of alone time where I didn't have to take care of anyone, so I could just rest. My dreams had diminished.* I wore myself down, trying to be everything for my family without caring for myself.

Both Bart and I felt resentment: he envied my staying home, while I longed to go to work. My life felt unbalanced, with too much time spent on others and not enough alone time or adult interaction. Days and months passed, and I just existed, with no goals or direction. And all it took was a shiny, new truck to change everything between us.

### *New Truck, New Him*

Bart had always worked hard to provide a good life for us, so when he wanted a new truck, I felt he deserved it. Despite his less-than-stellar credit, I didn't hesitate to put the truck in my name, knowing I could manage the payments. Just before Christmas one year, we visited the dealership, and Bart fell in love with a $50,000 truck. To make the monthly payments manageable, we needed to put down $15,000. I'd never spent that much on a down payment, but with gratitude for the life he provided for us, I wrote the check and wished him a Merry

Christmas. I was happy to be able to make that dream come true for him. However, my feelings soon changed.

Did I mention that Bart craved attention and validation, particularly from women? He wasn't a bad person, but he tended to prioritize his desires over others' needs. After getting the new truck, something in him shifted, and he began going to the gym every day, sometimes twice a day. He also joined four different softball teams.

I didn't understand his obsession until I discovered inappropriate text messages from a woman at the gym. This revelation left me questioning other aspects of our relationship, and I began to feel overlooked, unappreciated, and taken advantage of, slipping into a depression.

A friend of ours became a real estate agent, inspiring Bart to sell our house and buy a new one. We worked hard to improve his credit and prepare our home for sale. We found a seemingly perfect new house with all the amenities I'd ever dreamed of. From the outside, our life appeared perfect, and others envied our picturesque family and beautiful home. However, I felt unfulfilled and aimless. Seeking purpose, I decided to get my real estate license. I enjoyed the classes, passed the test, and eagerly anticipated a new chapter in my life. Little did I know, a harrowing experience lay ahead—one I wouldn't wish on anyone.

### *One of My Worst Fears Come True*

Six months after moving into our new house, everything changed. One day, as I was storing something in the attic, I opened the spare bedroom closet and discovered our daughter's winter clothes and jackets covered in a mysterious white substance. Panic surged through me. I had no idea what it was, but I instinctively knew something was terribly wrong. I laundered all the clothes, but the situation quickly escalated. Soon, I found tiny bites on my legs and experienced unsettling crawling sensations when putting on my pants. I was horrified.

Why did that horrify me? It's because one of my most paralyzing fears in life was bugs. The very thought of participating in those TV shows where people won money by allowing creepy crawlies to walk on them made my heart race. I was convinced I'd have a heart attack and die if I ever tried. My fear was colossal.

In a frenzy, I cleaned everything and called exterminators, researching extensively to understand what was happening. The house was only a few years old, and I was meticulous about cleanliness, so there wasn't a speck of dirt to be found. However, the exterminators couldn't find anything either, making me feel as if I was losing my mind. The situation continued to deteriorate. I'd take clothes out of the dryer, put on my pants, and instantly feel that unnerving crawling sensation. It was pure torture.

Desperate for relief, I followed an exterminator's advice to put ice in the dryer, hoping the steam would kill whatever was lurking inside. Sleep eluded me, my nerves frayed, and I hadn't slept well for weeks. I knew I needed to escape the house, so I planned a weekend getaway. One night, as I was cleaning my car and washing clothes after dark, I heard an ear-piercing screech, and something flew violently out of the dryer vent on the side of the house. I immediately called wildlife specialists to investigate, but they, too, found nothing and dismissed my concerns. I was on the brink of questioning my own sanity.

At that point, I couldn't take it anymore. I begged Bart to take me to the hospital. They put me in a room alone, and a doctor came in to ask me questions while Bart stayed in the lobby, chatting with a nurse. The doctor prescribed medication to help me relax and Benadryl in case I was experiencing an allergic reaction. I wondered if my chronic back pain from previous accidents, shoulder surgeries, and prescribed pain medications were exacerbating my ordeal or if I was living in a waking nightmare.

Bart thought I was going crazy, and honestly I would have thought the same thing if it were someone else. There were times that I questioned it myself. I was in a state of hypervigilance for months. The way I was cleaning and obsessing seemed "crazy" but due to the extent of my fear I didn't know any other way to handle the situation. I remember saying "I don't care where you take me, just get me out of here."

Thankfully, Curtis came to my rescue and arranged for me to go away for a little while. The Place was like a retreat and exactly what I needed at the time. I learned to breathe for the first time in my life. My nervous system was programmed to be in a constant state of fight or flight, so I had never learned how to relax my mind, or my body. They taught me meditation, diaphragmatic breathing, and weaned me off pain medication. I began to feel alive again.

One night while I was there, during a phone call with my daughter, I discovered she was with her father at another woman's house. The heartache was unbearable. There was nothing at that moment that I could do. So, I had no choice but to surrender it to God, asking for protection for my daughter, as

I stood there helpless. He knew I needed to be at a point of powerlessness to do that though. Had I been home I probably would have jumped in my car and tried to go find her. The next morning, during meditation, I asked God, "Why are You allowing this to happen?! My dream was to just have a family." All I heard was, *"He cannot go where I am taking you."*

That was not what I wanted to hear at all. I couldn't fathom a life without him, mainly because I was holding onto this ideal picture, and I never wanted my child to grow up without their mother and father together. Even though this broke my heart, I was in a rush to get home.

Returning home unannounced, I found Bart ready to leave me for someone else. My family sided with him, which really intensified the pain. Even though my heart was hurting I knew I had to be strong in front of him. So, when he told me that he found someone else and wanted me to move on, he didn't expect my calm acceptance of his decision. I looked at him and said, "Okay" and walked away.

Shortly after, I received a message from my first boyfriend in 6th grade, Jonathan. He somehow heard what was going on between Bart and I and said he was coming to take me to dinner. "Okay," I responded. I didn't know what else to say, I just wanted the pain to stop. When I wasn't there when Bart returned home, his jealousy flared. He apologized and confessed all of his wrongdoings, including flirting with the nurse at the hospital. The nurse, you ask?!

Yes, the nurse. The same one he spoke to at the hospital while I was being checked on. He admitted that he was exchanging numbers with her in the hallway as the doctors were seeing me. For some reason, I appreciated his honesty and believed he could change. His vulnerability was new to me, and I felt loved for the first time in a long time. I forgave him and decided to give our relationship one last chance.

Some people might think I was foolish, and at times, I felt that way too. But the fear of the unknown was greater than the fear of how I looked to everyone around me. I desperately clung to the hope that our family could remain intact and that Bart's newfound honesty and vulnerability would be the catalyst for lasting change.

Despite the overwhelming heartache and challenges I had faced, I did what I had always done and put them in a "this didn't happen" box. In other words, I disassociated with the incidents (until they decided to come back out). I chose to keep moving forward, determined to find a way to heal and build a better life for myself and my daughter.

### My "Ring Off" Moment

As the relentless bug issue in our home continued, I couldn't help but wonder why God would allow this to happen. I knew He loved and forgave me, so I knew that if He was allowing this to happen it was for a reason. The enigmatic phrase "he can't go where I am taking you" haunted my thoughts, making me feel like a stranger in my own home. One night, as I lay in bed, I whispered a fervent prayer: "God, I feel like you're telling me to leave, but I have no idea where to go or what to do. If you are, can you please show me a sign? Like a really big sign, so I can't miss it."

*The very next day*, as I drove through the city of Wilmington, Delaware, I came across a sight that I would have never expected: a man resembling Santa Claus standing on the corner of a rough street downtown, holding a 6-foot cross. Yes, 6-feet tall! His presence was made even more striking by the enormous RV parked nearby, emblazoned with the words "Jesus freak." I couldn't help but pull over and approach this stranger - knowing it had to be my sign.

After asking him so many questions at once, he smiled warmly and explained, "I'm in town because I'm going to a convention in Philadelphia where some of the biggest apostles and evangelists will be prophesying and praying over people."

Feeling an inexplicable connection to this man and the prayer I prayed, I knew I had to attend the convention. But who could I possibly ask to join me? My mind raced through the people I knew, but there was only one person who might understand: Delorse, my stylist. She was the only one that knew everything I was going through at the time, and she had a strong relationship with God so she was the least likely to think I was "crazy."

"Delorse, would you consider going with me to a convention in Philly?" I asked hesitantly when I called her, because Philly is not the safest place to go. "There will be people prophesying and praying over others, and I feel I really need to be there."

To my surprise and relief, she agreed without hesitation: "Yes, I'll go with you!"

At the convention, surrounded by music and friendly faces, Delorse and I found ourselves in line to be prophesied over. As my turn approached, my stomach fluttered with a mixture of excitement and nerves. I stepped forward into a circle of apostles and closed my eyes, ready to listen to what God wanted to tell me.

One of the apostles, Apostle Dave, spoke with his strong and gentle voice, "I see the struggles you've faced, the mistreatment you've endured, and the longing in your heart for something more." He paused, then said something I never anticipated: "Take off your ring."

What?! I hesitated, feeling a whirlwind of emotions and uncertainty. I didn't want to give up my dream of my children growing up with both of their parents together. Sensing my resistance, Apostle Dave continued, "You have two choices: you can stay where you are and live a 'mediocre' life or take off your ring and lead tens of thousands of women to freedom."

"Whoa." I didn't know what that would look like, or even what it meant, but I did know one thing for sure: I did not want to stay where I was. With my heart pounding, I knew what I had to do. *RING OFF!*

Another woman joined in, her voice soothing. "I see you in a field of green grass, surrounded by mountains." "Where is that?" I responded. "Follow the Holy Spirit", she said.

Unsure of what to do next, I did the only thing I could think of: search Google to find a place that has "green grass and mountains." I scoured the internet for hours. When I discovered Bell Roper Mountain in Greenville, South Carolina, I thought to myself, *this must be it*, especially when my lease was approved based on my credit history alone without having to prove a source of income (which I didn't even have at the time).

I approached Bart with the idea of starting over in South Carolina. Reluctantly, he agreed, and we planned for my daughter and I to move first while he sold the house in Delaware. Although our relationship had deteriorated into a mere semblance of roommates, I clung to the hope that if we were meant to be then maybe this would bring the change we needed. Regardless of the outcome, I knew I had to follow the path laid before me, as it seemed to be the only way to discover the life I was meant to live.

As I packed our belongings, I felt a mixture of anxiety and anticipation. Bart, on the other hand, seemed increasingly distant. Despite our initial agreement, I couldn't shake the feeling that he wouldn't follow through with the move. Regardless, I knew I had to trust the guidance I had received and forge ahead.

### *I Knew I Was NOT Crazy*

As the day of departure drew near, I could feel a knot of fear tightening in my stomach. Amidst the whirlwind of emotions, I knew I had to make one last effort to discover the truth behind what was going on in our house. I decided to call in an environmental specialist for a final inspection.

Two ladies arrived, and I found myself recounting the entire ordeal yet again. I braced myself for their skepticism, expecting to hear another "We can't find anything," like I'd heard so many times before. But to my relief and surprise, these women actually took my concerns seriously.

As they headed up to the attic, one of the ladies gasped. "Oh my goodness. Hand me a Q-tip," she exclaimed. Turning to her partner, she requested a small vacuum tool.

She looked me in the eyes, her expression grave. "You had a really bad bat infestation. The previous owners nailed an opening shut, but they never dealt with the issue. There's guano all over the rafters, and it's extremely harmful to breathe in."

As if that wasn't bad enough, she continued, "They leave a scent that attracts other bats in the area. Since they can't get into the attic anymore, they've been entering through the dryer vent. What about the bugs, I asked. "Well, here's the thing," she replied. *"Bats carry bugs."*

My stomach dropped, and I felt sick. A wave of nausea washed over me, but at the same time, a sense of relief flooded through my body. The agonizing search for answers was finally over and the best part was: "I *wasn't* crazy."

I then called the insurance company, desperate for guidance on how to proceed. I was physically, mentally, and emotionally drained from the nightmare that had become my life. I just wanted to leave, to get as far away as possible. But the thought of driving nine hours to a new place I've never been before with my three-year-old daughter terrified me, creating a whirlwind of negative questions swirling through my mind only feeding my fear.

I became more emotional at that point, seeking to confide in Bart about my fears and doubts, secretly hoping he would make them go away. To my surprise, he actually encouraged me to go. Deep down, I knew something wasn't right. My instincts told me that he had met someone else, but at that point, I couldn't care enough to stay. I was beyond done with the house and everything that had transpired within its walls.

As the insurance adjuster finished writing up the claim details in the driveway, he remarked, "If this happened to me and my family, my wife would have burned the house down." My level of "done" reached such an intense high that as he said that, I thought to myself, *If the house were to go up in flames at this very moment, I could stand here and watch everything I have ever worked for burn without a care in the world.*

That thought just ensured that I needed to close this chapter of my life. That moment when you know you need to make a leap, but you're not sure how you will muster up the courage to actually jump. That was me, at that moment. I can still feel that knot in my stomach, full of nerves and uncertainty.

The next morning, as I grappled with my fear of everything that could go wrong, Bart called to inform me that my mom and his mom were heading to the courthouse, trying to prevent me from taking our daughter so far away. He urged me to leave before they could stop me. It was then that I realized God was stepping in, doing for me what I couldn't do for myself.

With that extra push, I finished packing our belongings, and off we went.

I wish I could say that this marked the end of the worst season of my life, but unfortunately, that wasn't the case. Things got even worse before they started to get better, as I'll explain in the next chapter. The lesson I want to impart here is that no matter how terrible things may seem, God allows life to happen for us, not to us. He loves us too much to leave us in places that we do not belong. We can get caught up in our hardships and not realize that everything is happening for our greater good.

Though it felt like life was working against me during that time, it was actually guiding me towards growth and self-discovery. I had been stubborn, holding on to things and people much longer than I should have. If I had possessed the self-worth, confidence, or courage that comes from truly loving oneself, I would have left much sooner. I would have also purchased that property when I had the chance, sparing myself much of the pain recounted in the next chapter.

In the end, it's essential to remember that adversity often leads to growth and strength. By recognizing that God allows life to happen for us and not to us, we can weather even the darkest storms and emerge stronger on the other side.

## *The Fourth Step*

As we journey through life, we must not only embrace new stories about ourselves but also adopt new ways of being. I found God, yet I continued to settle for my old habits and patterns because *my dreams were so small.* That is not what He wants for us. He wants us to have life, and have it more abundantly.

This leads us to the fourth step to going from unloved and unwanted to fully loved and admired: *make the courageous decision to give up your plans for a "Greater One".* It is there where you get to trade your small dreams and prayers for ones that are beyond what you could even ask or think. When you step into His will, and what is possible in this life, He will take you to places you can't even imagine being in.

Just as I had my 'ring off' moment to give up my old, mediocre life for the purposeful life God wanted for me, now is the time for *your* 'ring off' moment. What does that decision look like for you? What is God asking you to release, surrender, or walk away from?

What is your "Ring Off Moment?"

It doesn't have to be a monumental decision like moving to another state. It could be choosing to love yourself, ending a toxic relationship, or breaking free from self-doubt or an addiction of some sort. If you're ready to have your own 'ring off' moment, answer the following questions:

1.  Reflect on the moments when you've settled for less than you should have. What are the relationships or situations that you are settling in right now in your life? What is holding you back from embracing your "ring off" moment?

    _____

    _____

    _____

    _____

2.  What is the one major change or decision God is nudging you towards? What is He asking you to let go of? What is that "thing" that *cannot* go where He is taking you?

    _____

    _____

    _____

\*\*\* Close your eyes and place your hands on your heart (you can stand up for this if you'd like). Imagine it is this exact day a year from now and ask yourself where are you in your life? What room are you walking in, who is there and what did you leave behind to get there?

3.  In the context of your "ring off" moment, you must cultivate ways to increase your self-love and self-worth. This will help you to make decisions that align with your true purpose and happiness. List 3 things that you can do on a daily basis to assist you in this process.

    _____

    _____

    _____

    _____

*\*\*\* Every morning when you get out of the shower, set the timer on your phone for two minutes. Stand there naked, look at yourself in the mirror and say to yourself (out loud) "I love you and you're beautiful". This will help you to fall in love with yourself on a visceral level. "It takes 120 days to rewire your brain, so count your days. If you miss*

one, *start over."* This *small exercise will change the way you see and feel about yourself.*

4.  It's very important to have a support system around you that encourages and uplifts you as you navigate through the challenges and uncertainties of your life-changing "ring off" moment. What church and or group can you get involved with (in your area) that can give you wisdom, and direction?

_____

_____

_____

_____

*\*\*\* I recommend finding a Christian or non denomination church because I believe your journey with God should be based on a personal relationship with Him. "Not a religion".*

*My favorite church is called "The Journey" in Newark Delaware, and their subline is "A Real Church for Real People". It is very modern and they go above and beyond for the community. I believe church should feel like a home, warm and welcoming. They have so many different groups and activities that they do for anyone that wants to join. They even have groups for the children. They take them on trips and do things that I have never known a church to do. It truly is special and my prayer is that they have "The Journey" (church and concept) in every major city across America, potentially even global.*

*Unloved*

# Self-Love To Self-Worth

I thought that when I left, everything would magically fall into place and get easier. But that's not what happened. "You know the saying 'it gets harder before it gets easier'? Well, that's definitely what happened here," I muttered to myself. I never could have imagined what was about to happen; it almost didn't feel real.

My daughter and I finally arrived at Bell Roper Mountain, and they quickly showed us to our apartment. When I walked in, it didn't feel right – in fact, it felt really wrong. The furniture was minimal and really cheap. There was a small two-person couch, a coffee table, and a queen bed in one bedroom. There was no bed for my daughter, and it didn't feel like a place I could call home.

Standing in that apartment, I was overridden with fear and emotions. I felt like I'd made a terrible mistake. "I'm scared, really scared," I whispered to the empty room. I tried to go back up to the office and talk to someone, but they were already closed for the day.

I called Bart, hoping he would say, "Just come back."
Not because I wanted to go back to him, but because I wanted
something or someone that I knew. I felt homesick. My
emotions were running wild. He didn't answer the phone for a
while, and when he called back, he encouraged me to stay, which
hurt me even more.

I really wanted any excuse to run back to what was
familiar, even though it was slowly killing me inside. I say that to
shed light on how our brains operate and how our minds are
designed to protect us, often doing the complete opposite. You
see, if I had run back, I would still be in the same place I was
internally at that time, if not worse. Thankfully, God loved me
too much to let that happen. He honored my 'ring off' moment
more than I did.

With Bart being short and dismissive with me over the
phone, I cried myself to sleep that night, and the next day, I went
back to the office, hoping they would let me out of the lease I
had just signed (because I signed it without seeing the place first).
I had no idea where I would go or what I would do; I just knew
that the apartment was not where I wanted to be. To my
surprise, they didn't let me leave. They did, however, let me
choose another apartment – one that felt a little more
comfortable.

It had a fireplace and a balcony that wasn't on the first floor. It was a lot better than the first one, so I was grateful for that. Moving into an empty apartment, I was scared and unsure of what to do. I called Bart for help, but he refused and even closed our joint bank account.

Desperate, I went to a furniture store and broke down in tears. The store employee kindly offered a 72-month interest-free loan, so I picked out a bedroom set I'd always dreamed of. They only charged me a fraction of what it should have cost.

After signing an incorrect invoice, I debated whether to correct the mistake or see it as a blessing. Ultimately, I decided to do the right thing and returned to the store to sign the correct invoice. I questioned what I was doing because signing those papers would hold me liable to another $3,000.00. In my confusion, I backed into the trailer attached to my car, denting my Escalade.

At that moment, I felt a wrenching gut check. I knew I needed to go in that store and sign those papers, no matter how scared I was. I felt so lost and alone. Even though I knew God was real and I believed He told me to go down there, I didn't have a strong relationship with Him yet, and He felt very far away. Looking back now, He was there the entire time. He showed up in the furniture store. He sent movers that would go above and beyond to help me unpack the U-Haul and even show me around the city. Something just wasn't right.

It didn't feel like home. I was still full of fear and uncertainty. I read the Bible, looking for some answers and what I should do next because I was so lost. I remember calling my mom, crying and saying, "I didn't think I would miss you so much, but I do."

She was apologetic about how she treated me before we left and said that she saw another side of things and wished she hadn't treated me the way she had. That felt comforting, at least a little. "At least I have her," I told myself.

I tried to find a church down there and get more involved in the area. The people were really nice; it just wasn't "home". I was constantly battling fear and uncertainty, but I knew I had to keep pushing forward. I leaned on my faith, and as time went on, I began to adapt to my new surroundings.

Slowly, I started making connections in the community. The fear and uncertainty never completely went away, but they became less overwhelming as the days passed.

### _Surprise, Surprise!_

One morning, while my daughter happily watched Dora the Explorer and ate her cereal a loud knock on the door interrupted us. To my surprise, it was a police officer. "Bart's at the front desk with a court order, trying to take your daughter from you," he informed me.

"WHAT?!" I exclaimed, bewildered. "Are you kidding me? How is that even possible? He sent us down here!" I explained my reasons for leaving and the officer assured me that legally he could not take her from me. His exact words were, "You picked a good state", because he would have to come to South Carolina to fight you for custody.

Even though I felt betrayed, I was grateful that he was there, so I allowed him to visit with our daughter. And when they met, she ran to him, shouting, "Daddy, Daddy!" Overcome with emotion, we all teared up. We went to the park, but Bart soon announced that he had to leave. My daughter and I cried, and even Bart shed tears as he pulled away. I could not even begin to know at that moment how much worse things would get.

After he left, I called my mom to tell her what had happened. She revealed that a letter from Family Court had arrived for me. With my permission, she opened it and discovered that it was a notice for an Emergency Ex-Parte Hearing. Bart had accused me of kidnapping our daughter and taking her to South Carolina without his knowledge or consent. I dropped the phone in disbelief. "You can't be serious," I said to her. "Oh, I'm pretty serious," she replied.

Desperate to return for the court date, I packed our belongings, rented a U-Haul, and put everything in storage, knowing we wouldn't be back for a while. My daughter and I returned to the place I'd tried so hard to escape. I reached out to my mom's friend, Mary, hoping she would go with me for support. I did not want to go in there alone and I was terrified of losing my daughter. Mary couldn't accompany me to court, but she gave me invaluable advice: "You don't have to go alone, Take God with you." Those words gave me a sense of peace and security.

With God by my side, I went to the courthouse early on the day of the hearing. I sought help from the public defender's office, where a woman listened to my story and reviewed Bart's false accusations against me. She forwarded my information to the public defender attorneys, but I knew I wouldn't have representation that day.

As the hearing approached, my sadness turned to anger. In the courthouse hallway, I encountered Bart, his mother, and their attorney. They expected me to be late, but I defiantly informed them that I'd been there all morning.

As we waited in the hallway of the courtroom waiting for our case to be called, I sat as far away from them as possible, and prayed. I asked God to take control of the situation and reveal the truth. Despite my nerves and lack of legal representation, I had faith that God would not let the lies win, and that the truth would prevail. Yet, walking into the courtroom, knowing my daughter's future lay in someone else's hands, I couldn't help but feel a lingering sense of fear.

## ***Breakthrough In The Courtroom***

The courtroom's clock ticked away the minutes until, at last, my name echoed through the hallway. I swallowed deeply, stood up, and entered the courtroom, my heart pounding in my chest. Bart and his lawyer walked to the right while I veered left. His mother wasn't allowed inside—a relief at first, but as the hearing unfolded, I wished she'd been there to witness the truth.

The judge, clad in her black robe, read the papers before her, her voice solemn and authoritative. "Do you agree with these allegations?" she inquired, her eyes piercing through me.

"Absolutely not, Your Honor," I replied, my voice unwavering. "I have documentation proving that those allegations are not true."

I couldn't help but wonder if Bart had truly written those terrible things or if it was his attorney's interpretation. Regardless, it pained me to repeat the false claims that I was losing my mind, imagining that there were bugs on me, and kidnapping our daughter to South Carolina without his permission.

Brandishing the insurance claim and the U-Haul receipt with Bart's signature, I presented my evidence. The judge, her eyes narrowed, asked him to confirm his signature and whether he had received the insurance claim money. To my relief, Bart admitted to both.

The judge's gavel struck, denying the emergency request and ordering us not to take our daughter out of state. She established a split custody arrangement and set a court date for a few months later. I couldn't help but wish Bart's mother had been in the courtroom since she only knew her son's version of events. Losing her was like losing a mother figure that I had respected and admired.

Later, as I scrolled through Facebook, I stumbled upon photos of an event Bart attended with a young, pretty girl. It had only been twelve days since I left and seeing him move on "publicly" so quickly was like a punch in the gut. My mind raced, worrying about our daughter and how this new woman might treat her. The worst-case scenarios played in my mind, and I couldn't shake the feeling of being replaced.

Determined to stop dwelling on the past, I reached out to the familiar face who I knew had always cared for me, Jonathan. He accepted my apology, for what had taken place a few months prior, and came to my rescue. We shortly ventured into a new relationship, but the new romance moved way too fast for me.

One night, as I prepared for my mother's birthday celebration, he wanted me to spend time at his place. I ended up "people pleasing" with him and upsetting my mom by being late on her special day. It was then that I knew I had to put an end to this cycle.

I called him and said, "I need to be alone. I need time to heal and focus on myself." Although it hurt him again, it was a necessary step for my healing process.

For the first time in a long time, I was done putting others before my own needs. The journey to rediscover myself and find solace in my own company had finally begun.

## *There Are No Coincidences*

Facing a lease dispute in South Carolina, I had no choice but to make a quick trip for a court date. Opting to fly out of the Philadelphia airport, I found myself early in the morning, bleary-eyed and weary, waiting in line to board my flight. That's when a man behind me caught my attention. I overheard him talking and saying something about real estate.

Turning around full of sudden energy, I introduced myself as a real estate agent and we struck up a conversation, connecting deeply right from the start. I have never connected with a man this quickly, and in such an intimate way.

We were seated across the aisle from each other on the plane. Our connection only grew stronger during the flight, as we spoke the entire two and a half hours. The flight attendants shot us disapproving looks as we leaned into the aisle, but we couldn't help ourselves. We were so engaged that we barely noticed the passing time.

Upon landing, I handed him my business card, fully knowing that our paths would cross again. He went off to a car auction while I proceeded to South Carolina for my court appearance. I couldn't help but feel that this was a divine connection, from the way he was standing right behind me in line, seated right next to me on the plane, and the way I have never experienced a connection like that before. I knew there was something special there and I would hear from him again.

As I arrived at Bell Roper, the attorney for the apartment complex managed to get the case dismissed due to a technicality: the name of the apartment complex didn't match the name of the company that owned it. Frustrated and disappointed, I had to refile the paperwork and wait for another court date.

Thankfully, the trip wasn't a waste, as I was invited to lunch later that week with Eric, the man I had an instant connection with on the flight. He was so nice and even brought me tulips. I knew there was something really special about him.

Unfortunately, after that, I felt the need to avoid seeing him for months because I found out something that would change my world forever.

## *Not One, But Two*

After staring at it for what felt like the longest couple of minutes of my life, a light purple line appeared. *I was pregnant!* And just then, I felt like the weight of the world had been placed on my shoulders. The overwhelming fear that gripped me was almost paralyzing. I agonized over how I would raise two children alone, how society would judge me for having children with two different fathers, and whether I could even provide a stable home for my growing family.

The whirlwind of all the events that had taken place in the last few months, and the fact that I had no income and the fear of failing as a mother I just wanted to die. My thought at that moment was *"God just kill me now. I can't do this."* Desperation and fear consumed me as I faced the seemingly insurmountable task of finding a place to live. Not to mention how I was going to take care of two children as a single mother. It was one of the first times I ever understood how my mother felt. As a realtor, I didn't have pay stubs, which made renting difficult. Tension with my mother was escalating, and I knew I needed to find a place for us to stay, sooner than later.

In a moment of despair, I broke down in my car and cried out to God for help. I said, "I know I'm supposed to trust You, but I don't know how. Please help me trust You." Miraculously, less than 2 hours after, I found myself on my mother's balcony, asking a man who was cleaning out his condo if he knew of any available rentals. To my surprise, he said the unit would be available in two weeks. After a heartfelt conversation, during which I explained my situation and my determination to provide a stable home for my children, he agreed to rent it to me for only $600 a month, waiving the security deposit.

This experience taught me that even in the darkest moments, there is hope and guidance if only we are willing to trust and let go. And if we don't know how all we have to do is ask.

## *The Comeback*

After a nearly traumatic labor, my son was born and slowly but surely, life began to improve. My mother moved in with her life partner, and I relocated to her condo upstairs. The extra space brought a sense of normalcy to our lives. My children finally had their own room, and I gained some much-needed privacy and personal space. Driven by the desire to give my children the life they deserved, I turned my pain into an unquenchable fire within.

My mother once told me, "You will rise from all of this like a Phoenix." Her words ignited my determination to rebuild my life. I knew what God put in my heart as well as the things spoken over me, and I knew deep down in my soul that there had to be so much more. Although I wasn't an avid Bible reader, I found guidance in the sermons of Joyce Meyer and Joel Osteen. I devoted myself to learning, growing, and healing from the pain I endured. I was tired of losing and hurting all the time.

As I embarked on this journey, I reconnected with Eric, the man I had met on the airplane. We stayed connected through text and he always wanted to meet with me, but I avoided that by saying I was busy, when really I was just ashamed of the fact that I was pregnant.

After months of avoiding him due to my pregnancy and fear of judgment, I was finally ready to meet him now that the baby was here. We agreed to meet for lunch. He carried himself with such pose and confidence, which I found very attractive. As

we sat down, I spoke up, saying, "I have something to tell you."
Surprised, he replied with, "I have something to tell you as well."
I decided to let him go first.

He opened up about a bad decision he had made:
entering into a relationship with someone after I had pushed him
away when we first met on the plane. I listened attentively, and
then it was my turn to share my confession. I told him about my
pregnancy and how I was embarrassed and afraid he would judge
me. I expressed the real reason why I had avoided seeing him for
months – my pregnancy, using the excuse of being too busy to
cover it up.

He was incredibly understanding and gracious about it,
which left me feeling grateful, and very relieved. It was a rare
experience to have someone be so understanding, and it touched
my heart deeply.

Following our lunch, he invited me to his home. When
we pulled up to the gate, I thought to myself, *"this is your house?!"*
As we walked through this exquisite masterful work of art,
feelings of unworthiness flooded my heart. Despite my growing
feelings for him, I knew I needed to heal and rebuild myself
before pursuing a relationship. As tough as it was, I courageously

chose to focus on me. We maintained a friendship, and I told him that I had to believe if it was meant to be, it would be.

## *My Transformation Journey*

After making that courageous decision to focus on healing before jumping into a relationship, I became even more committed to rising. I immediately cut out distractions and unhealthy influences even if that included family members. Choosing to only focus on personal growth. I read, wrote, and listened to empowering messages all day, every day.

During one of the messages, Joel Osteen said a line that created massive change in my life, and in the life of others God would use me to impact: "The way to stop hurting is to help someone else." Because I was so determined to stop hurting and heal, I took his advice and started a Facebook group called *Empower*. I posted positive messages, and I shared the positive lessons I had learned in hopes to help others heal, and in turn it helped my healing in the process.

During this transformative period, I was showing a house to a client and I met the owner of the house while I was there, which is rare. After speaking to Jamison, the owner of the house, he did something unexpected—he walked out to his car, retrieved a book and handed it to me. "Read this," he said with a knowing smile. I thanked him and planned to read it at my leisure. But Jamison had other plans, "You should finish it in two weeks, tops," he said, setting an ambitious deadline that sparked my determination.

The next morning, he texted me, asking what page I was on. His accountability fueled my motivation to read and complete the exercises within this book, *Think and Grow Rich* by Napoleon Hill. That book changed my life. It taught me the power of visualization and faith, prompting me to dream big and trust that God will provide everything I need along the way, I just have to do my part.

A month later, a unique opportunity presented itself. My doctor was launching a new company and needed someone to manage it. Despite my lack of medical background, I seized the chance, confident in my ability to learn and adapt. The deal was: as the company grew, so did my income. Because of that, I was determined to make it grow.

Remembering the lessons from the book, *Think and Grow Rich*, I then set my sights on my dream car – a Range Rover. Even though I was only making $600 a week at that time and the price was $90K for one, I trusted in God's provision. He has always allowed me to have a luxury car at a reasonable price. I would find something a few years old that still looked brand new. So, I said, "God, if it's Your will, please let me find one I can afford."

I visited several dealerships, test driving models with varying sticker prices. Each car offered a different experience, but none felt quite right.

After searching diligently, I found the perfect vehicle at a fraction of its original cost. It was a V8 Supercharged Range Rover with a third-row seat and TVs in the headrests for my kids, just as I had envisioned. Located in West Chester, PA, it was priced at $35k, making it more affordable than any of the others I had seen.

When I went to see it, it was inside on the showroom floor. I instantly fell in love. The payments were $598 a month, and I knew in my heart that this was the one. It's important to note that I'm not advocating for purchasing an expensive car that one cannot afford; rather, I'm emphasizing the importance of developing a strong relationship with God and trusting in His guidance with your every step.

The original sticker price for that car was $98k, and though it was a few years old, it still looked, drove and felt brand new. Within six months of reading *Think and Grow Rich*, I had manifested my dream car and secured a job for which I didn't technically "qualify" for. Just as the book described.

This journey of growth and transformation was marked by unforgettable encounters – Jamison's gift of *Think and Grow Rich* changed the way that I saw things and opened my doors to receive the beautiful gifts that life has to offer us. I strongly encourage you to get that book and read it after this one. Just as in this book, the exercises and questions it asks are of the utmost importance, so answering them will determine your outcome.

### *Your Fifth Step*

As I delved deeper into self-discovery and healing, one of the truths that radically changed my life on my transformation journey was when I learned that our subconscious mind operates 95% of the time. My jaw dropped at this realization – *95% is practically 100%*. This fact was startling because our subconscious mind governs our way of being, our thoughts, our responses to situations, and the culmination of our life experiences.

I knew mine was in dire need of transformation, an entire reprogramming. That's when I began exploring ways to reprogram your subconscious mind and found a lot of helpful videos on YouTube. I discovered that even when we're asleep, our subconscious mind remains active. You can literally reprogram it while you sleep just by letting one of the videos play next to you. I found this to be amazing. I would just pick one every night depending on whatever I was feeling that day and hit play.

Why is this important? Because the fifth step to going from unloved and unwanted to fully loved and admired is to *reprogram your subconscious mind to increase your self-worth*. This step in the process will change the trajectory for you and your family. It's the step where you eliminate everything that doesn't serve you and choose healing and growth over everything, especially entering another relationship.

Regardless of whether the other person is different or not, if you don't heal yourself, you'll end up hurting those closest to you – your spouse and your children. We've all been guilty of this at some point, but our loved ones deserve better, as do we. When that happens, you end up fulfilling the saying: "If you don't heal what hurt you, you'll bleed on the people that didn't cut you."

Many people struggle with this step because our minds convince us that we need someone to be there for us and will tell us things like we deserve to be loved. If you find yourself in this mindset, I ask you this question, "Can what that person is offering you be truly characterized as *love*?" We attract what we are, so often the person you attract is just as unhealthy, if not more, than you. My heart aches for those who don't give themselves this precious gift, as they end up spending their lives in relationships with people incapable of loving them the way they deserve. The same goes for men, too. The truth is that the love we so desperately seek is inside of us, and we cannot truly love anyone until *we first learn to love ourselves.*

As I reflect on my journey, I am grateful for the remarkable people I've met and the lessons I've learned. Like the Phoenix, I rose from the ashes, fueled by faith, determination, and a relentless desire to give my children the life they deserved.

But I would not have the amazing life that I have today if I did not reprogram my subconscious mind to increase my self-worth. God wanted to bless me so much, but if I did not shift my thinking, and way of being, I would not have been able to receive His gift. I would have ruined it because I would have brought all of my unhealed trauma into my future and pushed people away in the process.

He wants to give you the desires of your heart, but He doesn't want you to ruin your blessings when you receive them.

### ***30-Day Unloved To Fully Loved Challenge***

This exercise will be different because it doesn't end within this book. In fact, I'm going to introduce you to the *30-Day Unloved To Fully Loved Challenge* where you're going to follow these five steps for the next 30 days so you too can reprogram your subconscious to increase your self-worth and receive all that God really wants to give you.

Step one: Create a morning routine that fills and centers you. Rise a few minutes earlier to spend some quiet time in reflection, embracing the possibilities of the day ahead. Read something uplifting - I personally recommend a daily prayer or devotional book. Engage in a heartfelt conversation with God, share your thoughts and desires, seek His guidance, and express gratitude for His blessings in your life.

Step two: Fuel your morning with motivational wisdom by listening to inspiring speakers like Joyce Myers, Joel Osteen,

TD Jakes, Tony Robbins, and others as you shower and prepare for the day. Let their words empower and encourage you to face each day with renewed purpose and determination.

*Don't forget your 2 minutes in the mirror.

Step three: Purge all negativity from your life. Turn off the television (especially the news) and eliminate negative influences (radio, conversations, etc.) for these next 30 days to protect your mind. Surround yourself with positivity, opening your mind to transformative ideas and perspectives.

Step four: READ, READ, READ. Unleash the power of the written word to change your life. *Think and Grow Rich* by Napoleon Hill and *Next Level Thinking* by Joel Osteen are just two of the many books that inspired me. Numerous other gems await your discovery. Create a reading list of at least five to ten books you're going to read and embrace that book list as a catalyst for growth, even if you've never considered yourself a reader. Remember, you don't have to enjoy something to benefit from it – just dive in. The minimum we should read everyday is 30 minutes.

Step five: Reprogram your subconscious mind every moment you have, whether asleep or awake. Listen to reprogramming videos on YouTube as you sleep, selecting a new one each night. Explore affirmation videos or search for specific topics to heal or manifest in your life. The content you absorb during the day will also contribute to your reprogramming process, so choose wisely what you allow into your mind.

By reprogramming my subconscious mind to increase my self-worth, I emerged. I did more than just rise like a Phoenix, I rise to my "worth." This transformation didn't just change me; it opened the door for God's abundant blessings to flow freely into my life. As you embark on the *30-Day Unloved To Fully Loved Challenge*, trust in the power of these steps, and embrace the limitless possibilities that await you. When you truly love and value yourself, you become a beacon of light, attracting the love and the life that you truly desire.

# The Rise

I was no longer consumed by shame and guilt. I felt lighter and held my head higher, finally understanding who I was and, more importantly, Whose I was. For the first time in my life, I was proud of myself. It wasn't just about my monetary accomplishments; it was about the "Rise." I needed to prove to myself that I was not weak, that I could rebuild and overcome everything that had come against me.

My deep-rooted desire to be strong and powerful stemmed from my childhood when I couldn't fix or control anything. I admired bold, confident women and their powerful presence. Initially, I just wanted to rise from the ashes like a Phoenix, but as I chose to get "better" rather than "bitter" and let God guide me, He took me on an inward journey.

During our conversations, God showed me how to not just rise from the ashes, but to "Rise To My Worth." He taught me through His word, other people, and our intimate experiences that I was *already* everything I had always strived to be. He showed me that I could trust Him, that He would always make a way for me, and taught me the true depth and meaning of being integral.

There were times when my character was tested, like when I was undercharged for something or received extra money. I knew these seemingly small moments were tests of my character. He wanted to know if I would always do the right thing; and when I did, He rewarded me, greatly.

For example, one time at Christmas, I bought several Yankee candles to give as gifts. They were "buy one, get one free." When I got home, I realized that they hadn't charged me for one of the candles. Instead of keeping it, I called the store to let them know. The employee thanked me for my honesty and wished me a Merry Christmas. Later, a technician installing a filtration system told me they wouldn't charge me for the $10,000 system due to paperwork errors. This happened right after my call to the store. That's how God works; if He can trust us with a little, He can give us a lot.

Living with this conviction has profoundly impacted my life and helped build my self-confidence. The more I did the right thing, even when no one was watching, the more worthy and self-assured I felt. The more time I spent with God, the more I heard His voice in my spirit, guiding and encouraging me. My church calls this practice a "slot and spot." It's about setting aside a specific time and place to connect with God. The more you seek Him, the closer He gets to you. It works exactly like any other relationship in our lives: *the more you nurture it, the more it grows.*

I am far from perfect, but I am worth so much more than I ever knew, and so are you. God knows my heart, and because I love Him so much and choose to seek Him daily, He anoints and protects me. I see life as a journey where I am God's beloved child, and if someone does something wrong to me, they are doing something wrong to Him. When I walk in this truth, I can live without fear of anything. I can face challenges head-on, knowing that I am never alone and that God is always by my side. The knowledge and wisdom I have gained through this journey, along with the unconditional love that I now know and feel, are priceless.

### ***Preparing Us For Each Other***

As things improved with the company I worked for and I began making more money, I found a bigger house for myself and my children. It had enough bedrooms and even a home office, which I needed since I ran the company from home until it grew large enough to hire more staff.

On the outside, everything seemed perfect, but on the inside, parenting my strong-willed children alone was getting harder. When COVID hit and my daughter had to attend school online, the situation worsened. She wasn't learning, and I couldn't sit with her during the day to teach her since I had to work to provide for them.

One evening, I sat in my living room, where I often read. Instead of reading, I began a heartfelt conversation with God. "God, this is really hard, and I need help," I said. "I never wanted to do this parenting thing on my own. Where is my husband?" The response I received was clear: "*I'm preparing him for you.*" I hoped it wouldn't take too long, as I was known to be quite the handful. I'd never been the quiet or submissive type, likely because I'd never felt safe enough to be so. I was passionate about the things dear to my heart, unafraid to speak my mind and stand up for myself.

However, my journey had taught me that there were many times when it was best to keep quiet. I still stood up for what was right, but I'd learned to do it lovingly. In difficult situations, I'd ask God to speak for me and through me, because I wanted to be a good example of His perfect love.

Left to my own devices, I could become frustrated, irritated, overwhelmed, and anxious, which I didn't like. If you're honest with yourself and ask what you need to learn, work on, or see within yourself, you'll receive the answers. The more you seek, the more you'll see.

Upon asking the questions "What am I supposed to learn here?" and "What are you trying to teach me?", I received a notification about a book club hosted by someone I knew. They were reading *The Four Agreements*, a book recommended to me several times. Recognizing this as a sign from God, I eagerly joined the book club.

While discovering the principles within the pages, I found the concept of "not taking anything personally" particularly enlightening.

I discovered so many things about myself. One of the biggest truths I learned was this: It's amazing how we create stories in our minds about people or situations, and most of the time, *they're not even true.*

As I delved deeper into the book, I learned how our childhood experiences shaped our perceptions and actions as adults.

I learned more about how our brains work, and I knew I needed to grow and gain more knowledge to become the woman and wife God was calling me to be. I also learned to truly "become her," I had to "be her" *now* - acting like her in every part of my life. I couldn't wait for things to change to step into that "Royal" Megan. This meant dressing like her, walking like her, and talking like her, but more importantly learning to handle problems like her (with grace and kindness).

For me, this also meant being kind over being right, leading with love, and understanding that people's actions are often shaped by their pain and past experiences. I had to learn to trust God and be loving, no matter what others did or didn't do for me.

God waits for us to be ready and willing to accept the blessings He has for us. His love for us is so strong that He won't give us gifts before we are ready. Just like you wouldn't give a ten-year-old child a car and tell them to start driving, God knows the perfect timing for each of His blessings in our lives. This idea is reflected in a Bible verse, Proverbs 20:21, which says, "An inheritance obtained too early in life is not a blessing in the end." We need to be prepared for the blessings God has in store for us.

As we grow and change, we become ready for the blessings God has for us, and only then can we truly be happy and become the people we were meant to be. Let this encourage you to keep growing and learning, knowing that as you do, you open the doors to a life full of amazing blessings.

## *Listening To The Call*

I embarked on a journey of self-discovery and growth, aiming to become the woman and wife God desired for me. I began practicing the qualities I wanted to embody, such as kindness, love, and understanding different perspectives.

During this period of personal transformation, I felt a strong urge to reach out to Eric, the man I met on the plane to South Carolina. I had always been too afraid to make the first move, but this time I texted him, "Do you want to meet me for a drink?" He agreed, and we met the next day.

At this point of my life, I had done so much work reprogramming my subconscious mind to elevate my self-worth that I felt like I belonged there. There were no longer any lingering 'confidence' questions that came up in my mind, like it did the first time I visited his home. Who I was now was a completely different person than who I was one year ago.

As I walked into the restaurant, I saw Eric sitting at a table near the bar. This time, the connection between us felt different – stronger. We talked for hours and planned another dinner together. At the end of the next dinner, he kissed me in the parking lot afterwards. I then stopped him and spoke up with courage.

"Eric, I really like you, and I don't want to play games," I said firmly. "I don't 'share' the person I'm with. I want someone who values and respects me."

He listened and seemed to understand. Soon after, he invited me to Florida with him. Our time there was magical – falling asleep watching the sunset and engaging in deep, meaningful conversations. He gently encouraged me to open up about my feelings, fears, and past experiences.

As our bond strengthened, I knew in my heart that Eric was the man God had intended for me. For the first time in my life, I felt truly safe and loved.

He was an incredible father, with two truly wonderful boys. He instantly bonded with my children, bringing a sense of order to our lives. He was everything I had prayed for and more: highly intelligent, successful, funny, and down-to-earth. His playful side brought joy, while his commanding presence instilled the respect my children needed. For me, having someone I could rely on and trust to help with the responsibilities was a breath of fresh air.

It was astonishing how much we had in common. Both of us had made similar mistakes in the past, and we shared the same desires and needs in a relationship. We connected on a profound level and got engaged within a few months. He proposed to me on a dock behind our Florida home, fireworks illuminating the night sky. Our life together felt as magical as that moment.

As a pediatric dentist, he had built one of the largest practices in the country, a testament to his brilliance and determination. Yet, despite his success, he treated everyone with kindness and respect, never acting superior. He understood that happiness comes from within, not from material possessions or social status.

Many signs indicated that our union was divinely orchestrated. He was fifteen years older than me, which I appreciated because it meant he had reached a level of maturity where he could prioritize others over himself. He knew there was always room for improvement, and we both believed in continuous growth.

### ***Let The Light In***

Throughout my journey, I learned to never consider myself as having "arrived." Instead, always be open to learning, growing, and evolving. I wanted to use my knowledge, wisdom, and experience to help other women heal, raise healthy children, and change the trajectory of their lives. Being with Eric inspired me to continue growing and pursuing my heartfelt desires. I had great ideas and wanted to achieve so many things but didn't know where to start. I prayed for God to bring the right people into my life, and guess what? He brought them.

One day, I came across a Facebook ad featuring a woman I'd never seen before: Tara Oldridge. She was spunky, beautiful, and I felt an instant connection. Although I had never paid for a coach, I knew I was meant to work with her. I attended her virtual event, signed up, and a month later, she hosted an in-person event at her house in Florida. When I told

Eric I wanted to go, he agreed and even accompanied me. I thought I would attend, gather the information I needed, and be done with paying Tara. However, she presented an offer I couldn't refuse, so I asked Eric to invest in me because I really wanted to work with her. It was more money than I had ever spent at once on anything, but I wanted to pay it in full to prove a few things to myself; my commitment to growth, to overcome a scarcity mindset, and to step into my full potential.

As part of the investment, I received leadership training through Tara's *Lighthouse Leadership Academy*. She emphasized the importance of marriage and encouraged Eric to join me. Without knowing what to expect, we both committed to the training. Leadership training is intense, designed to reveal your blind spots, push you beyond your comfort zones, and help you break through barriers. It also teaches emotional intelligence and strong leadership skills.

I'm incredibly grateful for the experience and for having Eric by my side. He even celebrated his birthday during that three-day training session, which speaks volumes about his character and dedication. Although he didn't need to participate, he did so because it meant so much to me.

When I heard the words from God, *"I am preparing him for you,"* I couldn't grasp the depth of that statement at first. But I began to understand that our connection was more intricate and detailed than I ever imagined. It was as if we were made for each other. He communicated with me in a way I had never experienced before. I used to hold everything in and try to figure things out on my own, but he made me feel safe and would ask questions to help me. He's a lot like me, wanting to fix things, but he has a calmness I admire and appreciate. I call it his superpower. No matter the situation, he always makes it better.

For example, shortly after we decided to give our relationship a fair chance, I was let go from the company I had built. We had hired a new director who didn't like me from day one. Eventually, she forced the owner to choose between her or me, and I had to go. I felt heartbroken and betrayed, but Eric offered to help. At first, I hesitated, but he insisted it was his job to take care of me and my kids as we were engaged. His support left me speechless, and I could only thank God. He has a unique way of getting me to open up and, once I do, he always finds a way to make things better.

That challenging situation turned out to be the best thing for us. Now, I had the flexibility to travel with Eric to Florida every week. He loves it there and would live there full-time if our kids didn't attend school in Pennsylvania, where we both grew up. Our life together is more amazing than I could have ever imagined. We share custody of our children, alternating weeks, and travel to Florida when the kids are with their other parents. We have created a perfect life that surpassed anything I could have ever imagined, and it all started with our divine meeting on that plane.

Since he proposed on the 4th of July, I wanted to get married on the same date the following year. I thought it would be a fantastic anniversary to celebrate moving forward. When discussing our wedding plans, Eric told me I could have any type of wedding I wanted.

Most people might choose an extravagant, over-the-top event, but I couldn't fathom spending so much money on a single day. Instead, I suggested we take our closest friends and family somewhere beautiful and exotic for a week to celebrate our union.

There were still COVID regulations in place, so we had to be mindful of where we would go. We researched various locations, eventually discovering the Half Moon in Jamaica. Upon visiting, we knew it was perfect and we set about making the arrangements.

We booked two villas for the week, ensuring our friends and family would be comfortable. Our villa was right on the water, providing the perfect backdrop for our wedding. We exchanged vows in the backyard, followed by dinner and dancing. We had a full staff all week - a chef, maid, and butler - and the wedding coordinator took care of every detail, allowing us to focus on our special day. All I did was pick the colors, flowers, and food, while they went above and beyond. We even had a violinist to play our song as I walked out and down the aisle. It was so beautiful and more special than I could have ever imagined.

When we got married, the kids and I moved in with Eric into our dream house in West Chester. This house was like something straight out of a movie, with every feature we could ever want and more. Our living space expanded from a 3,000 sq ft home to an incredible 23,000 sq ft home. The kids now enjoy a fantastic movie theater, game room, an infinity pool, and a pool house where my daughter, at just nine years old, pretends it's her apartment. They even have their own personal suite with a living room attached. I mean, come on – what more could you ask for?

And guess what the view from our bedroom in the master suite is? You guessed it, *green grass and mountains* – exactly like the word God gave me through that woman at the convention during my "ring off" moment. I could never have imagined living such an exquisite life. All I knew was that I wanted a gated driveway and a nice home, but this experience just goes to show that God's plans are always bigger and better than anything we could ever dream up. It truly brings to life the verse Ephesians 3:20 which says, "All glory to God, who is able through His mighty power at work within us, to accomplish infinitely more than we could ask or think."

There are many things I love about my husband, and one of them is his passion for shoes. He enjoys bidding on luxury women's shoes from high-end brands like Christian Louboutin, Gucci, and Giuseppe Zanotti. In our two main houses, one in Pennsylvania and the other in Florida, both closets are filled with incredible shoes.

I share this story because there was a time in my past when I lost everything materialistic, and losing my shoes hurt the most. I've always had a deep love for shoes and took great care of them. I remember asking God, "why is this was happening, *You* know I love my shoes?" In my heart, I heard a response, *"I will replace them with interest."* At the time, I had no idea what that would look like, but I knew I had to trust Him.

Not only has God replaced my shoes with interest, but He has also restored everything in my life *more* than a hundredfold. I share that in order to tell you this, "If He did this for me, He can do it for you."

### *Right People, Right Time*

As I embarked on this new journey, I encountered remarkable individuals who made a significant impact on me who God has used to come into my life at perfect times, such as Forbes Riley, Chantal Santiago, and Christian Santiago.

The first person, Forbes Riley, is a dynamic woman who specializes in teaching people how to perfect their pitch. In essence, she helps individuals present themselves in a powerful and confident way. She also coaches people on becoming confident on camera, among other skills. I've learned a lot from her, as have many others. Forbes shared a piece of advice during a training session that completely changed my life, and the life of my nine-year-old daughter, which I'll discuss in the conclusion.

The second person, Chantal Santiago, is a powerful woman I met through Tara Oldridge. Chantal conducts inner healing sessions, which are unlike anything I've ever experienced. Although I have a strong relationship with God, I didn't fully

*Unloved*

135

understand Jesus and the Holy Spirit. Chantal provided clarity on this topic and guided me through a healing journey where I confronted the lies I came to believe about myself. For example, as a child, I would hear comments like, "Who do you think you are?" and "She thinks she's special." These words led me to suppress my own light to avoid judgment. Chantal taught me how to break those agreements and *permanently* close those doors.

Lastly, Chantal's husband, Christian Santiago, is a faith-driven powerhouse with a special gift for writing books and leading Christian leaders. Our meeting was divinely orchestrated, and within minutes, I knew he was the one meant to help me with this book. While I can share my life story and make it "good," God wanted this book to be "great", so that's why He brought Christian into my life – he helped me greatly in bringing this story to life.

It was almost as if I continued to fill myself up with God's truth and positivity, I found His love within me growing exponentially. It was like I had made a complete exchange – I relinquished all that was harmful to me, allowing Him to guide me, and in return, I received all of my heart's desires. My heart swelled, overflowing with love and gratitude.

Learning that I don't need to earn my worth, because my worth was already established in God's eyes became a life-changing revelation. God desires our hearts, and He longs for us to become more like Jesus.

There is a wealth of wisdom within the Bible, yet so many people resist reading it – I, too, was once among them. Society has complicated and distorted the truth in countless ways, leading to confusion.

But let me simplify it for you: all paths to temporary relief ultimately lead back to the foundational spiritual principles found in the Bible. You have two choices: take the long, convoluted route riddled with obstacles and dead ends, or go directly to the source – our Father "God". He gave us an invaluable gift – the Bible, our Basic Instructions Before Leaving Earth (B.I.B.L.E.). Everything we need to prosper, heal, succeed, and experience freedom is within that book. He will give you everything you need – the people, places, and things – you need to create the life of your dreams. All you have to do is just step out of the way and let *Him* lead your life.

### *Your Final Step*

In my journey, I have encountered incredible individuals who have profoundly impacted my life and my family's. I have discovered the importance of community, emotional intelligence, leadership, and breaking free from the lies that bind us. I have learned to lean in when I see people who inspire me and remain a lifelong student, always seeking new ways to grow and learn.

As I share the resources and steps that have changed my life, I realize that God has placed these incredible people in my path to bring this life-changing guide to you – so that you, too, can realize the desires of your heart and share the story He has given you. Trust in the process, and everything will come together; the answers will reveal themselves.

Reflecting on my past, I now see that even the most challenging moments – like sharing custody of my children – were blessings in disguise. These experiences provided me with the quiet time I needed to study and learn, preparing me for the calling to become a leader. My heart's desire has always been to make a significant impact and live like a star. And as I asked questions and sought answers, I discovered that we truly become what we believe we are.

As we reach the end of this chapter, I urge you to remember that you are not alone on this journey. God has placed resources, mentors, and communities in your path to help you uncover your true worth, heal, and become the leader you were always meant to be. That's why the final step in going from unloved and unwanted to fully loved and admired is to *find people that have what you want, do what they did, and you'll get what they have.*

It's really that simple. The truth is we all come from the same place. We have the same God. We may have been dealt different hands but what is possible for *one* is possible for *all*. It is your job to believe it.

I have outlined the steps and resources that have been crucial in my journey that I know will be crucial for yours. May God guide you towards them as you embark on your own path of transformation:

1.   Get In A Life-Changing Community:
    a.   Changing the Trajectory
*https://www.facebook.com/groups/1609032849563877*
    b.   Empower
*https://www.facebook.com/groups/381900502500542*

*(*Get involved in a church family like The Journey*)*
*https://www.yourjourney.tv/*

2. Become A Powerful Leader:

3. Master Your Pitch:

    a.    Join Forbes Riley's community

    *https://www.forbesriley.com*

4. Experience Inner Healing:

    a.    Schedule an "Inner Healing Session" with
          Chantal Santiago

    *https://www.christianpsantiago.com/chantal*

5. Enhance Your Story And Expand Your Influence:

    a.    Schedule a connection call with Christian
          Santiago, Biblical Mentor / Elite Ghostwriter

    *https://www.christianpsantiago.com/ghostwriting*

And so, as the sun sets on this chapter of our journey, I leave you with the unwavering belief that you are capable of achieving greatness, and that the love within you will continue to grow and overflow, illuminating the path ahead for both yourself and those you touch along the way.

Remember to follow the steps, click the links, and join the communities that resonate with you. Embrace the transformation that awaits you, and know that your story, too, will be a beacon of hope and inspiration for others.

You are destined for greatness, and as you continue to grow and learn, you will find that the love within you will not only transform your life but also the lives of those around you. So, as we close this chapter, remember that the adventure is just beginning. Embrace the unknown, lean into the challenges, and let your light shine brightly, for you are a beacon of hope in a world that so desperately needs it.

Together, we will rise, and together, we will change the trajectory of our lives, our families, and the world. Stand tall, be courageous, and let God's love within you guide you every step of the way.

# Conclusion

In the end, it truly doesn't matter where you come from, what you have been through, or where you may be at this very moment. We all originate from the same Source and possess the same power within us. It is what we *choose* to do that will determine our destiny. I believe the experiences we've had were necessary to shape and mold us into who we are called to be in this life.

For instance, my upbringing in poverty ignited a fire within me to rise above and show others that abundance and prosperity are accessible to all. It's simply a matter of a mindset shift and belief system. The closer you get to a new way of being, the more abundant your life will become. I always knew I was meant for a grand, abundant life because the desire and belief that it was possible for me never wavered.

Growing up feeling unloved and unwanted was part of my journey to discovering that the love I was always seeking resides within all of us, as it comes from our Source, our Creator. Once I was able to feel that love from Him, I truly loved myself and those around me, becoming the woman I was created to be.

However, *it's never just about us*. I was created to become this woman to help millions of people on my journey, but as mothers, I believe raising our children is the most important job of all. When we are unhealed, we unwittingly harm our children, but when we heal and learn to lead with love, we raise incredible individuals in the process.

Our children look up to us and aspire to be like us. Remember how I mentioned that one thing Forbes Riley said to me that changed my life? It was this: *include your children in your work*. If they approach you while you're working, don't dismiss them and make them feel less important; instead, explain what you're doing and let them absorb it. She said that she brought her children to work with her all the time, and now they run her company.

This changed everything for me because I began to let my daughter sit with me as I wrote and worked on this book, and guess what happened? She got into trouble at school one day, and I encouraged her to use her time in her room to create something amazing. "Go write a book or something. Use this time to create something magical." I said to her. The very next day, she called me and said, "Mommy, I wrote a book." Shocked by the whole thing, I had her read it to me. When she read it to me, I cried.

I knew it was something divinely inspired by God that was placed on her heart to help children everywhere. From that point, I knew we needed to get it published. Her book, titled "*You Are Loved*," reminds children of how loved they truly are and that anything is possible if they just believe in themselves.

She teaches them gratitude, affirmations, how to cope with sadness, tap into their creativity, and dream big. She even encourages them to write their own stories. All this, and she's only nine years old!

If you have children or know a child, I strongly encourage you to give them the priceless gift of her special book, "*You Are Loved*" by Mia'Bella "Lovie" Baylson is available on Amazon. It's an invaluable treasure that far outweighs anything else out there.

I share this with you to show you the realm of possibilities, and more importantly, to demonstrate what God wants to do in your life. He wants you to heal so that you can change the trajectory for yourself and your family. Every generational curse, He wants to break. Every generational wound, He wants to heal. Everything He did for me, He will do for you.

The life you have right now, He wants to give it to you abundantly without stopping. But there's one mission you must commit to in the process and that mission is *to love*.

For if love is the oxygen of the heart, and since God is love, then we can never truly live without Him. Embrace the power of love, let it heal you, and through that healing, use the power of love to change the world around you. In this profound realization, we find our purpose and the driving force to make an impact in the lives of those around us, especially our children.

As you reach the end of this book, let the emotions that arise within you serve as a catalyst for change, transforming not only your life but the lives of those you hold dear. This journey has only just begun, and as you take each step forward, remember that love is your guiding light.

We are all capable of greatness, but it is the power of love that will guide us there. So, as you turn the final page and embark on your journey of transformation, do so with the knowledge that *you are loved*, you are powerful, and you have a divine purpose in this life. Hold onto that truth, for it is the key to unlocking a world of boundless possibilities.

With tears in my eyes, as I celebrate you and how far you've come already, I invite you to join me in creating a legacy of *healing*, *hope*, and **love**, for yourself, your children, and generations to come. Leaving behind this kind of legacy is so dear to my heart because I know what it's like to feel unloved, and no one deserves to feel that pain.

So, this is my prayer for you:

*Father, thank You for the precious heart that is reading this right now. Thank You for using me, and my story to remind them of who You are and the power that they have ~ through You. Thank You for showing them through me and my life what is possible. Thank You for what You are igniting inside of them right now, and thank You for all of the amazing things that they will create in this world as they embark on their journey to change the trajectory for themselves, and their family. In Jesus' precious name I pray ~ Amen.*

# Never Forget

You were created to live the life of your dreams, but nothing great is accomplished alone. I would love to support you further on your journey. If you are ready to "Rise To Your Worth", you can reach out to me directly below:

https://risetoyourworth.net/

I Love You…

*Love always,*

*~Megan*

*Unloved*

# About The Author

Megan Lis Felix is a certified Love Coach and "Healing Agent" on a mission to empower millions of women to heal, transforming their pain into power and unlocking the purposeful life God has planned for them. Drawing from her own inspiring journey from abuse to abundance, Megan has already guided hundreds of women towards the deep healing they've always longed for.

Fueled by this mission, she leads people to freedom through three distinct avenues: her two Facebook Groups, *Empower* and *Changing The Trajectory*, and her coaching company, *Rise To Your Worth*.

*Rise To Your Worth* is devoted to supporting women on their journey of self-discovery and growth. With extensive experience in life coaching and hands-on life experiences, Megan has mastered the essential lessons required to overcome internal struggles and shift the attraction process, allowing her clients to thrive in healthy, loving, and amazing relationships.

Her individualized, positive approach helps clients attain their goals and set them on the path to achieving the life they've only dreamed of.

As a professionally trained and experienced life coach, Megan possesses the tools, understanding, and knowledge necessary to guide clients in creating the life they know exists but are uncertain they can attain. Megan is here to show you that not only is this life attainable, but you are also more than worthy of receiving it.

Committing to *Rise to Your Worth* is a significant step that requires dedication and a new belief system. Megan is committed to providing you with accountability, understanding, resources, and tools to transform your entire self into the amazing, beautiful, confident, loving, and powerful person you were created to be. She guarantees her unwavering support every step of the way.

If you're ready to rise to your worth and embark on a life-changing journey, connect with Megan Lis Felix. Together, you can unlock the abundant life and love that awaits you.

https://risetoyourworth.net/

Printed in the USA
CPSIA information can be obtained
at www.ICGtesting.com
JSHW011614061023
49620JS00006B/30

9 781733 403047